Dedication

To all those who ever struggled with learning a foreign language and to Wolfgang Karfunkel

Also by Yatir Nitzany

Conversational Spanish Quick and Easy

Conversational French Quick and Easy

Conversational Italian Quick and Easy

Conversational Portuguese Quick and Easy

Conversational German Quick and Easy

Conversational Dutch Quick and Easy

Conversational Norwegian Quick and Easy

Conversational Danish Quick and Easy

Conversational Russian Quick and Easy

Conversational Ukrainian Quick and Easy

Conversational Bulgarian Quick and Easy

Conversational Polish Quick and Easy

Conversational Hebrew Quick and Easy

Conversational Yiddish Quick and Easy

Conversational Armenian Quick and Easy

Conversational Romanian Quick and Easy

Conversational Arabic Quick and Easy

CONVERSATIONAL SPANISH QUICK AND EASY SERIES

The Most Innovative Technique To Learn the Spanish Language

BOOK - I, BOOK – II, BOOK - III

YATIR NITZANY

Copyright © 2021
Yatir Nitzany
All rights reserved.
ISBN-13: 978-1-951244-56-9
Printed in the United States of America

Foreword

About Myself

For many years I struggled to learn Spanish, and I still knew no more than about twenty words. Consequently, I was extremely frustrated. One day I stumbled upon this method as I was playing around with word combinations. Suddenly, I came to the realization that every language has a certain core group of words that are most commonly used and, simply by learning them, one could gain the ability to engage in quick and easy conversational Spanish.

I discovered which words those were, and I narrowed them down to three hundred and fifty that, once memorized, one could connect and create one's own sentences. The variations were and are *infinite*! By using this incredibly simple technique, I could converse at a proficient level and speak Spanish. Within a week, I astonished my Spanish-speaking friends with my newfound ability. The next semester I registered at my university for a Spanish language course, and I applied the same principles I had learned in that class (grammar, additional vocabulary, future and past tense, etc.) to those three hundred and fifty words I already had memorized, and immediately I felt as if I had grown wings and learned how to fly.

At the end of the semester, we took a class trip to San José, Costa Rica. I was like a fish in water, while the rest of my classmates were floundering and still struggling to converse. Throughout the following months, I again applied the same principle to other languages—French, Portuguese, Italian, and Arabic, all of which I now speak proficiently, thanks to this very simple technique.

This method is by far the fastest way to master quick and easy conversational language skills. There is no other technique that compares to my concept. It is effective, it worked for me, and it will work for you. Be consistent with my program, and you too will succeed the way I and many, many others have.

The Spanish Language
Spanish originated in Spain, and it closely resembles Portuguese, as both are Latin in their derivation and are therefore considered Romance languages. The Spanish language was spread during the 1500s by Spanish colonialists coming from Spain to South America. Since then, the language has grown and is now the fourth most-spoken language in the world. Spanish is still rising in popularity, as it has 98 million non-native speakers and 402 million native speakers. Don't you want to be a member of the ever-growing population of Spanish speakers? Now you can be, if you follow the simple instructions of this program.

CONTENTS

The Spanish Language 8
Memorization Made Easy 9
Reading and Pronunciation in the Spanish Language 10

Spanish – I 11
Introduction to the Program 12
The Program 15
Building Bridges 37
Verb Conjugation 41
Other Useful Tools in the Spanish Language 42

Spanish – II 45
Introduction to the Program 46
Travel 48
Transportation 51
City 53
Entertainment 57
Foods 61
Vegetables 65
Fruits 67
Shopping 69
Family 73
Human Body 75
Health 77
Emergencies and Natural Disasters 81
Home 85

Spanish – III 91

Introduction to the Program 92
Office 94
School 97
Profession 101
Business 103
Sports 107
Outdoor Activities 109
Electrical Devices 111
Tools 113
Auto 115
Nature 117
Animals 121
Religion, Holidays, and Traditions 125
Wedding and Relationship 129
Politics 131
Military 135

Basic Grammatical Requirements of the Spanish Language 140
Congratulations, Now You Are On Your Own 146
Note from the Author 148

The Spanish Language

Spanish originated in Spain, and it closely resembles Portuguese, as both are Latin in their derivation and are therefore considered Romance languages. The Spanish language was spread during the 1500s by Spanish colonialists coming from Spain to South America. Since then, the language has grown and is now the fourth most-spoken language in the world. Spanish is still rising in popularity, as it has 98 million non-native speakers and 402 million native speakers. Don't you want to be a member of the ever-growing population of Spanish speakers? Now you can be, if you follow the simple instructions of this program.

Memorization Made Easy

There is no doubt the three hundred and fifty words in my program are the required essentials in order to engage in quick and easy basic conversation in any foreign language. However, some people may experience difficulty in the memorization. For this reason, I created Memorization Made Easy. This memorization technique will make this program so simple and fun that it's unbelievable! I have spread the words over the following twenty pages. Each page contains a vocabulary table of ten to fifteen words. Below every vocabulary box, sentences are composed from the words on the page that you have just studied. This aids greatly in memorization. Once you succeed in memorizing the first page, then proceed to the second page. Upon completion of the second page, go back to the first and review. Then proceed to the third page. After memorizing the third, go back to the first and second and repeat. And so on. As you continue, begin to combine words and create your own sentences in your head. Every time you proceed to the following page, you will notice words from the previous pages will be present in those simple sentences as well, because repetition is one of the most crucial aspects in learning any foreign language. Upon completion of your twenty pages, *congratulations*, you have absorbed the required words and gained a basic, quick-and-easy proficiency and you should now be able to create your own sentences and say anything you wish in the Spanish language. This is a crash course in conversational Spanish, and it works!

Reading and Pronunciation

The pronunciation of Spanish, in comparison to the English language, is more or less the same. There are, however, a few exceptions that are listed below. Please read and familiarize yourself with the rules of Spanish pronunciation.

CE is pronounced as "se." *Él dice* is pronounced as "él di-se."
G when followed by *e* or *i* sounds like the letter *h* in English, like "hot." For example, *general* is pronounced as "he-nere-ral."
H is silent. For example, *hacer* is pronounced as acer
J is pronounced similar to the *ch* in German and in Hebrew ("loch," "channuka," and "yacht"). For example, the English word "garden", translated *jardin* in Spanish, would sound like "chardin." The sound is a little difficult to pronounce for non-Spanish speakers. Tip: pronounce as if you are coughing up phlegm in the back of your throat. The English word "job", translated *trabajo*, is pronounced as "tra-ba-cho."
Ñ is pronounced as "ny." For example, "morning," *mañana*, sounds like "ma-ny-ana."
LL is pronounced as "je." For example, "to arrive," *llegar*, sounds like "je-gar." However, in some Spanish countries, they pronounce it as "ye"; *llegar* would be pronounced as "ye-gar."
RR is hard to pronounce for non-Spanish speakers, but an easy
Tip is that the pronunciation is similar to the sound of a starting car engine, "rrrrrr." "Dog," *perro*, would be pronounced as "pe-rrrr-o."
V is pronounced as "b." *Victor* would be pronounced as "Biktor."
Z is pronounced as "s." For example shoe, *zapato*, would be pronounced as "sapato."

Conversational Spanish Quick and Easy
The Most Innovative Technique to Learn the Spanish Language

Part - I

YATIR NITZANY

Translated by:
Semadar Mercedes Friedman

Interior Design:
Menachem Otto

Introduction to the Program

People often dream about learning a foreign language, but usually they never do it. Some feel that they just won't be able to do it while others believe that they don't have the time. Whatever your reason is, it's time to set that aside. With my new method, you will have enough time, and you will not fail. You will actually learn how to speak the fundamentals of the language—fluently in as little as a few days. Of course, you won't speak perfect Spanish at first, but you will certainly gain significant proficiency. For example, if you travel to Spain or South America, you will almost effortlessly be able engage in basic conversational communication with the locals in the present tense and you will no longer be intimidated by culture shock. It's time to relax. Learning a language is a valuable skill that connects people of multiple cultures around the world—and you now have the tools to join them.

How does my method work? I have taken twenty-seven of the most commonly used languages in the world and distilled from them the three hundred and fifty most frequently used words in any language. This process took three years of observation and research, and during that time, I determined which words I felt were most important for this method of basic conversational communication. In that time, I chose these words in such a way that they were structurally interrelated and that, when combined, form sentences. Thus, once you succeed in memorizing these words, you will be able to combine these words and form your own sentences. The words are spread over twenty pages. In fact, there are just nine basic words that will effectively build bridges, enabling you to speak in an understandable manner (please see Building Bridges, page 37). The words will also combine easily in sentences, for example, enabling you to ask simple questions, make basic statements, and obtain a rudimentary understanding of others' communications. I have also created Memorization-Made-Easy Techniques (See page 9) for this program in order to help with the memorization of the vocabulary. Please see Reading and Pronunciation (Page 10) in order to gain proficiency in the reading and pronunciation of the Spanish language prior to starting this program.

My book is mainly intended for basic present tense vocal communication, meaning anyone can easily use it to "get by" linguistically while visiting a foreign country without learning the entire language. With practice, you will be 100 percent understandable to native speakers, which is your aim. One disclaimer: this is *not* a grammar book, though it does address minute and essential grammar rules (see Basic Grammatical Requirements of the Spanish

Introduction to the Program

Language, Page 140). Therefore, understanding complex sentences with obscure words in Spanish is beyond the scope of this book.

People who have tried this method have been successful, and by the time you finish this book, you will understand and be understood in basic conversational Spanish. This is the best basis to learn not only the Spanish language but any language. This is an entirely revolutionary, no-fail concept, and your ability to combine the pieces of the "language puzzle" together will come with *great* ease, especially if you use this program prior to beginning a Spanish class.

This is the best program that was ever designed to teach the reader how to become conversational. Other conversational programs will only teach you phrases. But this is the *only* program that will teach you how to create your *own* sentences for the purpose of becoming conversational.

Note to the Reader

The purpose of this book is merely to enable you to communicate in Spanish. In the program itself, you may notice that the composition of some of those sentences might sound rather clumsy. This is intentional. These sentences were formulated in a specific way to serve two purposes: to facilitate the easy memorization of the vocabulary *and* to teach you how to combine the words in order to form your own sentences for quick and easy communication, rather than making complete literal sense in the English language. So keep in mind that this is *not* a phrase book!

As the title suggests, the sole purpose of this program is for conversational use *only*. It is based on the mirror translation technique. These sentences, as well as the translations are *not* incorrect, just a little clumsy. Latin languages, Semitic languages, and Anglo-Germanic languages, as well as a few others, are compatible with the mirror translation technique.

Many users say that this method surpasses any other known language learning technique that is currently out there on the market. Just stick with the program and you will achieve wonders!

In order to succeed with my method, please start on the very first page of the program and fully master one page at a time prior to proceeding to the next. Otherwise, you will overwhelm yourself and fail. Please do *not* skip pages, nor start from the middle of the book.

It is a myth that certain people are born with the talent to learn a language, and this book disproves that myth. With this method, anyone can learn a foreign language as long as he or she follows these *explicit* directions:

* Memorize the vocabulary on each page.
* Follow that memorization by using a notecard to cover the words you have just memorized and test yourself.
* Then read the sentences following that are created from the vocabulary bank that you just mastered.
* Once fully memorized, give yourself the green light to proceed to the next page.

Again, if you proceed to the following page without mastering the previous, you are guaranteed to gain nothing from this book. If you follow the prescribed steps, you will realize just how effective and simplistic this method is.

The Program

Let's Begin! "Vocabulary" (Memorize the Vocabulary)

I - Yo / **I am** - Yo Soy, estoy
Are you - Tu eres, estas
He / she - Él / Ella
With you - Contigo / **With him** - Con él / **with her** - Con ella
With us - Con Nosotros
For you - Para Ti
Without him - Sin él
Without them - **(masculine)** Sin Ellos / **(fem)** Sin Ellas
This - Este, Esta, esto, **(p)** estas, estos / **This is** - Esto es / **Is** - Es, esta
Always - Siempre
Was - Estuvo, era
Sometimes - Algunas Veces / a veces
Maybe - Tal Vez / Quizás
From - De

Sentences from the vocabulary (now you can speak the sentences and combine the words).

Are you at the house?
¿Estas en la casa?
Sometimes I go without him.
A veces me voy sin él.
I am always with her.
Estoy siempre con ella.
I am from Spain.
Yo soy de España.
Are you from South America?
¿Eres de Sur América?
I am with you.
Estoy contigo.
Are you alone today?
¿Estás solo hoy?
This is for you.
Esto es para ti.

*This isn't a phrase book! The purpose of this book is solely to provide you with the tools to create your own sentences!

*Concerning *yo soy, estoy / es, esta* & *tu eres, estas*, please refer to the *permanent and temporary* section (page 141).

You – (**informal**) Tú / (**formal**) usted
I was - Estuve / estaba
Good - Bueno / **Better -** Mejor
Happy - Feliz
Here - Aquí
Now - Ahora / **Later, After -** Luego / Despues / Más tarde
Tomorrow - Mañana
The - El (m) / La (f) / Los (m)(pl) / Las (f)(pl)
Same - Mismo / Igual
It's - Es / Esta
And - y (pronounced as *ie*)
Between - Entre
If - Si / **Yes –** Sí / **Then -** Entonces
Also / too / as well - También

I was home at 5pm.
Estuve en casa a las 5 p.m.
Between now and tomorrow.
Entre ahora y mañana.
It's better to be home later.
Es mejor estar en casa más tarde.
If this is good, then I am happy.
Si esto es bueno, entonces estoy feliz.
Yes, you are very good.
Sí, eres muy bueno.
I was here with them.
Yo estuve aquí con ellos.
You and I.
Tú y yo.
The same day.
El mismo día.

*For pronunciation of *ñ*, refer to Reading and Pronunciation (See page 10)

*Concerning *estar* and *ser*, refer to the Permanent and Temporary section (See page 141)

*Too is *también*. However, "too much" is *demasiado*. "I am too tired" / *estoy demasiado cansado*.

*In Spanish, the plural form of "you", regardless of whether formal or informal, is *ustedes*.

Me - Me, mi *(read footnote below)*
Where - Dónde
Somewhere - Algun Lugar
There - Allí
Ok - Ok / bien / bueno
Even if - Aunqué
Everything - Todo
What - Qué
Almost - Casi

Even if I go now.
Aunqué si me voy ahora.
Where is everything?
¿Dónde está todo?
Maybe somewhere.
Tal vez en algún lugar.
What? I am almost there.
¿Qué? Estoy casi allí.
Where are you?
¿Dónde estás?
This is for us.
Esto es para nosotros.

---

*For pronunciation of the *ll* in *allí*, please refer to Reading and Pronunciation (See pg. 10)

*In Spanish, the pronouns *me*, *mi*, and *mí* could be quite confusing. *Me* signifies "myself" and is accompanied with direct and indirect objects as well as with reflexive verbs. *Mi* means "my." *Mí*, signifying "me," is used for the purpose of prepositions.
* Direct object—*El me habló*
* Indirect object—*Ella me dijo*
* Reflexive verb—*Yo me llamo*
* Adjective—*Es mi primo*
* Object of preposition— *Esta casa es para mí*

Without us - Sin nosotros
Son - Hijo / **Daughter** - Hija
Car – Auto, automóvil, coche, carro / **House** - Casa / **Home** - Hogar **Good morning** - Buenos Días
How are you? - Cómo estas?
Where are you from? - ¿De dónde eres?
What is your name? - ¿Cómo te llamas? / ¿Cuál es su nombre?
How old are you? - Cuantos años tienes?
Today - Hoy
Hello - Hola
Hard – Difícil / Duro
In – En / **At** - En el, en la
Already - Ya
Very - Muy

She is not in the car, so maybe she is still at the house?
Ella no está en el auto, entonces quizás ella está todavía en la casa?
I am in the car already with your son and your daughter.
Ya estoy en el auto con tu hijo y tu hija.
Good morning, how are you today?
¿Buenos días, cómo estás hoy?
Hello, what is your name?
Hola, cómo te llamas?
How old are you?
¿Cuántos años tienes?
This is very hard, but it's not impossible.
Esto es muy difícil, pero no es imposible.
Where are you from?
¿De dónde eres?

*Please refer to Reading and Pronunciation for pronunciation of *j* in *hija* (See pg. 10).

*"How old are you?"/ *cuantos años tienes*, literally means "how many years do you have?"

*In Spanish, the phrase "it's not" is flipped around—*no es* or *no esta*.

*"What is your name?" is ¿*Cómo te llamas*? However, you can also say, ¿*Cuál es su nombre*? which translates to "which is your name?"

*In the Spanish language, to signify the possessive adjective "your," we use *tu*, plural *tus*. However, the formal case of "your" is *su*, plural *sus*.

The Program

Thank you - Gracias
For – Para, por / **In order to** - Para
Day - Día / **Yesterday** - Ayer
Time - Tiempo
Since - Desde, hace / **Before** - Antes
No, not - No / **I am not** - Yo no estoy, yo no soy
That - **(M)** Ese, **(F)** Esa / **It's** - Es
But - Pero
Away - Lejos
Similar - Similar / mismo
Anything - Cualquier cosa
Other / Another - Otro
Side - Lado
Until – Hasta / **Still** - Todavia

Thank you Kenneth.
Gracias Kenneth.
It's almost time.
Es casi el tiempo.
I am not here, I am far away.
No estoy aquí, estoy distante (far)/lejos.
That house is similar to ours.
Esa es una casa similar ala nuestra.
I am from the other side.
Soy del otro lado.
But I was here until late yesterday.
Pero estuve aquí hasta tarde ayer.
Since the other day.
Desde el otro día.

*In Spanish, the definition of *de* is "of" or "from." However, in the event that the article "the" follows "of" or "from" (*de*) (for example, "from the" or "of the"), the *de* + *el* merges into *del*. This case applies solely to the masculine article *el*. If *de* is followed by the feminine article *la*, you can't say *del*, only *de la*. The same applies with plurals (i.e., *las flores del jardin, las flores de los jardines, la maestra de la escuela, el maestro del colegio, el maestro de los colegios,* etc.).
However, when someone says, *Ella es del Canada* or *Juan es del Peru*, many people would simply say, *Ella es de Canada* or *Ella es de Peru*. The *del* is used only because the names of these countries are also *El Canada* and *El Peru*. There a few others such as *El Congo*, etc. You can also use the merging of *de* + *el* in a sentence such as *la enfermera del hospital central*.

To be - Estar / Ser
I say / I am saying - Yo Digo / Estoy Diciendo
To see - Ver / **I see, I am seeing -** Yo veo / estoy viendo
I want - Yo quiero / **I need -** Necesito
I go – Yo voy / **I am going -** Me voy
What time is it? - Qué Hora es?
Without you - Sin Ti
Everywhere - Todo Lugar / cada lugar / todas partes
With - Con
My - (Singular) Mi / **(Plural)** Mis
Cousin - Primo
Right now - En este momento / ahora
Night - Noche / **Light -** Luz
Outside - Afuera
That is - Eso es
Any - Cualquier

I am saying no!
Estoy diciendo no!
I say no.
Yo digo no.
I want to see this during the day.
Yo quiero ver esto durante el día.
I see this everywhere.
Veo esto en todas partes.
I am happy without any of my cousins here.
Estoy feliz sin cualquier de mis primos aquí.
I need to be there at night.
Necesito estar allí por la noche.
You have to be at home.
Tienes que estar en casa.
I see light outside.
Yo veo luz afuera.
What time is it right now?
¿Qué hora es ahora?

*In Spanish, placing the pronoun "I" (*yo*) before a conjugated verb isn't required. For example, *I want to use this* is *quiero usar esto* instead of *yo quiero usar esto*. Although saying *yo quiero usar* isn't incorrect. The same rule also applies for the pronouns *you, he, she, them, we* (See page 143).

The Program

To wait - Esperar
To sell - Vender
To use - Usar
To know - Saber
To decide - Decidir
To find - Encontrar
To look for/to search - Buscar
To - A/ Al/ A la
Place - Lugar
Mall - Centro comercial
Easy - Fácil
Near – Cerca / Acerca
Between - Entre
Both – Ambos / Dos
That (conjunction) - Que

This place is easy to find.
Este lugar es muy fácil de encontrar.
I am saying to wait until tomorrow.
Yo digo hay-que (have to) esperar hasta mañana.
It's easy to sell this table.
Está fácil vender esta mesa.
I want to use this.
Quiero usar esto.
Where is the book?
¿Dónde está el libro?
I need to decide between both places.
Necesito decidir entre los dos lugares.
I need to know that everything is ok.
Necesito saber que todo está bien.
Is it possible to look for this book in the library?
¿Es posible buscar este libro en la biblioteca?
Is this place near?
¿Es este lugar cerca?

*"That" / "which" can also be used as relative pronouns. The translation in Spanish is *que*. "I need to know that everything is ok" / *Necesito saber **que** todo está bien.*

*In Spanish *a + el* becomes *al*. This only applies to masculine cases, however. For feminine cases, it's *a la*.

*This *isn't* a phrase book! The purpose of this book is *solely* to provide you with the tools to create *your own* sentences!

To look - Mirar
To buy - Comprar
To understand - Entender / Comprender
I do / I am doing - Yo hago / Estoy Haciendo
I can / Can I? - Puedo / ¿puedo?
Myself - Yo mismo / **Mine** - Mío
Them | They - (M) Ellos / (F) Ellas
Book - Libro
Food - Comida
Water - Agua
Hotel - Hotel
Problem / Problems - Problema / problemas
Enough - Bastante / Suficiente
Because - Porque
Why - Por qué
Like this - Así
Of - Del

I like this hotel because it's near the beach.
Me gusta este hotel porque está cerca de la playa.
I want to look at the view.
Quiero mirar la vista.
I want to buy a bottle of water.
Quiero comprar una botella de agua.
Do it like this!
Hazlo así!
Both of them have enough food.
Ambos tienen bastante comida.
That book is mine.
Ese libro es mio.
I have to understand the problem.
Tengo que entender el problema.
I have a view of the city from the hotel.
Yo tengo una vista de la ciudad desde mí hotel.
I can work today.
Yo puedo trabajar hoy.
I do what I want.
Hago lo que quiero.

The Program

To know - Saber
To work - Trabajar
To say - Decir
To go - Ir
I like - Me Gusta
Family / Parents - Familia / Padres
There is / There are - Hay
Who - Quien
Why – Porqué
Something - Algo
Ready - Listo
Soon - Pronto

I like to be at my house with my parents.
Me gusta estar en casa con mis padres.
Why do I need to say something important?
¿Por qué necesito decir algo importante?
I am there with him.
Estoy allí con él.
I am busy, but I have to be ready soon.
Estoy ocupado, pero tengo que estar listo pronto.
I like to work.
Me gusta trabajar.
Who is there?
¿Quien está allí?
I want to know if they are here.
Quiero saber si están aquí.
I can go outside.
Puedo ir afuera.
There are seven dolls.
Hay siete muñecas

*This *isn't* a phrase book! The purpose of this book is *solely* to provide you with the tools to create *your own* sentences!

To bring - Traer
To eat - Comer
To Drive - Manejar / conducir
With me - Conmigo
Without me - Sin mí
How much - Cuánto
Lunch - Almuerzo
Slow / slowly - Despacio
Fast / Quickly - Rápido
Inside – Adentro / dentro
Cold - Frío
Hot - Caliente
Were – Eran / estaban
When - Cuando
Only - Solamente (adverb) / sólo (adjective)
Instead - En vez
Or - O

How much money do I need to bring with me?
¿Cuánto dinero necesito llevar conmigo?
I like bread instead of rice.
Me gusta el pan en lugar de arroz.
Only when you can.
Solamente cuando puedas.
Go there without me.
Vete allí sin mí.
I need to drive the car very fast or very slowly.
Necesito manejar el auto muy rápido o muy lento.
Is it cold inside of the library?
Hace frío dentro de la biblioteca?
I like to eat a hot meal for my lunch.
Me gusta comer para mi almuerzo una comida caliente.

The Program

To answer - Contestar
To fly - Volar
To travel - Viajar
To learn - Aprender
To swim - Nadar
To practice - Practicar
To play - Jugar
To leave - Dejar
I go to - Yo voy a
First - Primer
Time / Times - Vez / Veces
Like (*preposition*) **-** Como
How - Cómo
Many/much/a lot - Mucho

I need to answer many questions.
Tengo que contestar muchas preguntas.
I want to fly today.
Quiero volar hoy.
I need to learn how to swim in the pool.
Necesito aprender cómo nadar en la piscina.
I want to learn how to play better tennis.
Quiero aprender a jugar mejor el tenis.
Everything is about the money.
Todo es sobre el dinero.
I want to leave my dog at home.
Quiero dejar a mi perro en casa.
I want to travel the world.
Quiero viajar por el mundo.
Since the first time.
Desde la primera vez.
The children are yours.
Los niños son tuyos.

* The feminine singular form of *mucho* is *mucha*, the masculine plural is *muchos*, and the feminine plural is *muchas*.

*With the knowledge you've gained so far, now try to create your own sentences!

To visit - Visitar
To meet - Conocer
To give - Dar
To walk - Caminar / Andar
Someone - Alguien
Us - Nosotros
Mom / Mother – Mamá / Madre
Nothing - Nada
Nobody - Nadie
Against - Contra
Which - Cuál
Just - Apenas
Around - Alrededor
Towards - Hacia
Than - Que

Something is better than nothing.
Algo es mejor que nada.
I am against him.
Estoy en contra él.
We go to visit my family each week.
Vamos a visitar a mi familia cada semana.
I need to give you something.
Necesito darte algo.
Do you want to meet someone?
¿Tú quieres conocer a alguien?
I am here on Wednesdays as well.
Estoy aquí los miércoles también.
You do this every day?
Haces esto todos los días?
You need to walk around the house.
Necesitas caminar alrededor de la casa.

*__Que__ could be translated into "what," "that, "than." To read more about the uses of *que*, (See page 142)

*In Spanish to signify "on" or "before" days, an *el* must precede the word. For example, on Wednesdays / *el miércoles*.

The Program

To show - Mostrar
To prepare - Preperar
To borrow - Emprestar
To look like - Parecer
To want - Querer
To stay - Quedar
To continue - Continuar
I have - Yo tengo
I have to - Yo tengo que
I must - Debo / yo tengo que (both can be used interchangeably)
I am not going - No me voy
Don't / Doesn't - No
Friend - Amigo
Grandfather - Abuelo
Way (road) - Camino
Way (method) - Manera
That's why - Por eso

Do you want to look like Arnold?
¿Quieres parecer a Arnold?
I want to borrow this book for my grandfather.
Yo quiero emprestar este libro para mi abuelo.
I want to drive and to continue on this way to my house.
Quiero manejar y continuar en este camino a mi casa.
I want to stay in Madrid because I have a friend there.
Quiero quedarme en Madrid porque tengo un amigo allí.
I am not going to see anyone here.
No voy a ver a nadie aquí.
I need to show you how to prepare breakfast.
Necesito mostrarte cómo preparar desayuno.
Why don't you have the book?
¿Por qué tú no tienes tu el libro?
That is incorrect, I don't need the car today.
Eso es incorrecto, no necesito el auto hoy.

---

*"To stay," *quedar*, however, "I want to stay in Madrid" becomes *quiero quedarme en Madrid*. The *me* becomes a suffix to the verb *quedar* since this is the reflexive case. To learn more about the reflexive form, please see page 144.

To remember - Recordar
To think - Pensar
To do - Hacer
To come - Venir
To hear - Escuchar
Your – Informal (S) Tu, **(P)**Tus/ **Formal (S)**Su, **(P)**Sus
Grandmother - Abuela
Dark / darkness - Oscuro / Oscuridad
Number - Número
Five - Cinco
Hour - Hora
Minute / minutes - Minuto / Minutos
A second - Un segundo
Moment - Momento
Last - **(M)**último /**(F)**última
More - Mas
About - Sobre

You need to remember your phone number.
Necesitas recordar tu número de teléfono.
This is the last hour of darkness.
Ésta es la última hora de oscuridad.
I want to come with you.
Quiero venir contigo.
I can hear my grandmother speaking Spanish.
Puedo escuchar a mi abuela hablando Español.
I need to think about this more.
Necesito pensar más en esto.
From here until there, it's just five minutes.
De aquí hasta allá, son solo cinco minutos.

To leave - Salir
To turn off - Apagar
To ask - Pedir
To sleep - Dormir
To stop - Parar / Detener
To take - Coger / Tomar
To try - Tratar
To rent - Alquilar
Without her - Sin ella
We are - Estamos / Somos
Spanish - Español
English - Inglés
America - America
United States - Estados Unidos
Airport - Aeropuerto
Permission - Permiso
Again - Otra vez / de nuevo

He must go and rent a house at the beach.
Él tiene que ir alquilar una casa en la playa.
I want to take the test without her.
Quiero tomar la prueba sin ella.
We are here for a long time.
Estamos aquí por mucho tiempo.
I need to turn off the lights early tonight.
Necesito apagar las luces temprano esta noche.
We want to stop here.
Queremos detenernos aquí.
We are from America.
Somos de america.
Your doctor is in the same building.
Tu doctor está en el mismo edificio.
In order to leave you have to ask permission.
Para salir tienes que pedir permiso.
I want to go to sleep.
Quiero ir a dormir.
Where is the airport?
¿Donde esta el aeropuerto?

To open - Abrir
To buy - Comprar
To pay - Pagar
To clean - Limpiar
To return (from place) - Regresar, volver
To return (an object) - Entregar
To hope - Esperar
To live - Vivir
Our - Nuestro
Without - Sin
Sister - Hermana
Nice to meet you - Es mi gusto cononcerte (it's my pleasure knowing you)
Name - Nombre
Last name - Apellido
Enough - Bastante
Door - Puerta
On - Encima de/ sobre

I need to open the door for my sister.
Necesito abrir la puerta para mi hermana.
I need to buy something.
Necesito comprar algo.
I want to meet your brothers.
Quiero conocer a tus hermanos.
Nice to meet you, what is your first name and your last name?
Es mi gusto conocerte, cuál es tu nombre y tu apellido?
We can hope for a better future.
Podemos esperar un futuro mejor.
It is impossible to live without problems.
Vivir sin problemas es imposible.
I want to return to the United States.
Quiero volver a los Estados Unidos.
Why are you sad right now?
¿Por qué estás triste en este momento?
Our house is on the mountain.
Nuestra casa esta encima de las montaña.

*This *isn't* a phrase book! The purpose of this book is *solely* to provide you with the tools to create *your own* sentences!

To happen - Occurrir
To order - Ordenar (demand), pedir (order an item)
To drink - Beber
To begin / To start – Comenzar / Empezar.
To finish - Terminar
To help - Ayudar
To smoke - Fumar
To love - Amar
To talk / to speak - Hablar
Child - (M) Niño / **(F)**Niña
Woman - Mujer
Excuse me - Permiso / Disculpa

This needs to happen today.
Esto tiene que ocurrir hoy.
Excuse me, my child is here as well.
Desculpe, mi niño está aquí también.
I want to order a soup.
Quiero pedir una sopa.
We want to start the class soon.
Nosotros queremos comenzar la clase pronto.
In order to finish at three o'clock this afternoon, I need to finish soon.
Para terminar a las tres de la tarde, tengo que terminar pronto.
I want to learn how to speak perfect Spanish.
Quiero aprender como hablar Español perfecto.
I don't want to smoke again
Yo no quiero fumar otra vez.
I want to help.
Quiero ayudar.
I love you.
Te amo.
I see you.
Te veo.
I need you.
Te necesito.

*To learn more about the typical uses of *te*, please see page 143.

*In Spanish, the definition of "to start/begin" can either be *comenzar* or *empezar*.

To read - Leer
To write - Escribir
To teach - Enseñar
To close - Cerrar
To turn on - Encender
To prefer - Preferir
To choose - Escoger / elegir
To put - Poner
I talk / I speak - Yo Hablo
Sun - Sol
Month - Mes
Exact - **(M)**Exacto/ **(F)**Exacta
Less - Menos

I need this book to learn how to read and write in Spanish.
Necesito este libro para aprender a leer y escribir en Español.
I want to teach English in Mexico.
Quiero enseñar inglés en Mexico.
I want to turn on the lights and close the door.
Quiero encender las luces y cerrar la puerta.
I want to pay less than you.
Quiero pagar menos que tú.
I prefer to put this here.
Prefiero poner esto aqui.
I speak with the boy and the girl in Spanish.
Hablo con el niño y la niña en Español.
There is sun outside today.
Hay sol afuera hoy.
Is it possible to know the exact date?
¿Es posible saber la fecha exacta?

*In the English language, adjectives precede the noun, but in Spanish, it's usually the opposite. "Big house" is *casa grande*, "new car" is *coche nuevo*, and "exact date" is *fecha exacta*.

*With the knowledge you've gained so far, now try to create your own sentences!

The Program

To exchange - Intercambiar
To call - Llamar
To sit - Sentar
Together - Juntos
To change - Cambiar
To follow - Seguir
Him / Her - Lo / La
Brother - Hermano
Dad - Papá
Sky - Cielo
Big - Grande
Years - Años
Up - Arriba
Down / below / under - Abajo, debajo
Of course - Por supesto
Sorry - Perdon
Welcome - Bienvenido
During - Durante
New - Nuevo
Never - Jamás / Nunca

I am never able to to exchange this money at the bank.
Nunca puedo intercambiar este dinero en el banco.
I want to call my brother and my dad today.
Quiero llamar a mi hermano y a mi papa hoy.
Of course I can come to the theater, and I want to sit together with you and with your family.
Por supuesto que puedo ir al teatro y quiero sentarme contigo y con tu familia.
If you look under the table, you can see the new rug.
Si miras debajo de la mesa, puedes ver la nueva alfombra.
I can see the sky from the window.
Puedo ver el cielo desde la ventana.
I am sorry.
Lo siento.
The dog wants to follow me to the store.
El perro quiere seguirme a la tienda.

*In Spanish an *a* usually precedes nouns relating to people or animals.

*In Spanish *a+el* becomes *al*.

To allow - Permitir
To believe - Creer
To promise - Prometer
To move - Mover (indicates motion) / mudar (switching locations)
To enter - Entrar
To receive - Recibir
To recognize - Conocer / reconocer
Morning - Mañana
Good afternoon - Buenas tardes
Good night - Buenas noches
People - Gente
Man - Hombre
Free - Gratis
Far - Distante
Different - Differente
Throughout - En todo
Through - A travéz
Except - Excepto

I need to allow him to go with us.
Necesito permitirle ir con nosotros.
He is a different man now.
Él es un hombre diferente ahora.
I believe everything except this.
Yo creo todo excepto esto.
Come here quickly.
Ven aquí rapido.
I must promise to say good night to my parents each night
Tengo que prometer decir buenas noches a mis padres cada noche.
I can't recognize him.
No puedo reconocerlo.
I need to move your cat to a different chair.
Necesito mover tu gato a una silla diferente.
They want to enter the competition and receive a free book.
Quieren entrar en la competición y recibir un libro gratis.
I see the sun throughout the morning from the kitchen.
Veo el sol por la mañana de la cocina.
I go into the house from the front entrance and not through the yard.
Entro a la casa de la entrada principal y no por el jardin.

*To learn more about the typical uses of *lo* and *la*, please see page 144.

The Program

To wish - Desear
To get - Conseguir / **To forget** - Olvidar
To feel - Sentir / **To like** - Gustar
Everybody - Todos
Person - Persona
Restaurant - Restaurante
Bathroom - Cuarto de baño
Goodbye - Adiós
See you soon - Hasta luego
Next (following) – Proximo / **Next** (near close) – Acerca / cerca
In front - Adelante, Enfrente / **Behind** – Atras / detrás
Bad - Mal
Although - Aunque
Great - Gran
Well - Bien

I don't want to wish you anything bad.
No quiero desearte nada mal.
I must forget everybody from my past.
Debo olvidar a todos de mi pasado.
I am next to the person behind you.
Estoy próximo a la persona detrás de ti.
To feel well I must take vitamins.
Para sentirme bien debo tomar vitaminas.
There is a great person in front of me.
Hay una gran persona adelante de mí.
Goodbye my friend.
Adios mi amigo.
Which is the best restaurant in the area?
¿Cuál es el mejor restaurante de la zona?
I can feel the heat.
Puedo sentir el calor.
I need to repair a part of the cabinet in the bathroom.
Necesito reparar una parte del gabinete en el baño.
She must get a car before the next year.
Ella tiene que conseguir un coche antes del próximo año.
I like the house, but it is very small.
Me gusta esta casa, pero es muy pequeña.

* "Wish you," *desear*, the verb, and the *te*, the object, connect. To learn more about the typical uses of *te*, see page 143.

To remove - Sacar
To hold - Mantener /Sostener
To check - Revisar
To lift - Levantar
Include / Including - Incluir /Incluyendo
Belong - Pertencer
Wood - Madera (construction) / leña (for burning)
Week - Semana
Beautiful - Lindo /Bello /Hermoso
Please - Por favor
Price - Precio
Small - Pequeño
Real - Verdad
Size - Tamaño
Even though - Aunque
It - **(M)** Lo / **(F)** La
So (as in *then*) - Entonces / **So** (so as in *so much*) - Tan/ tanto

She wants to remove this door please.
Ella quiere sacar esta puerta por favor.
This doesn't belong here, I need to check again.
Esto no pertenece aquí, necesito revisar lo otra vez.
This week the weather was very beautiful.
Esta semana, el clima estaba muy hermoso.
Is that a real diamond?
¿Es eso un verdadero diamante?
We need to check the size of the house.
Necesitamos revisar el tamaño de la casa.
I want to lift this.
Quiero levantar esto.
Can you please put the wood in the fire?
¿Puedes por favor poner la leña al fuego?
The sun is high in the sky.
El sol está alto en el cielo.
I can pay this although the price is expensive.
Puedo pagar esto aunque el precio es caro.
Including everything is this price correct?
¿Incluyendo todo, este precio es correcto?

Lindo /bello /hermoso is the masculine form of "beautiful, pretty." The feminine form is *Linda /bella /hermosa*. "Handsome" is *guapo*.

Building Bridges

In Building Bridges, we take six conjugated verbs that have been selected after studies I have conducted for several months in order to determine which verbs are most commonly conjugated, and which are then automatically followed by an infinitive verb. For example, once you know how to say, "I need," "I want," "I can," and "I like," you will be able to connect words and say almost anything you want more correctly and understandably. The following three pages contain these six conjugated verbs in first, second, third, fourth, and fifth person, as well as some sample sentences. Please master the entire program up until *here* prior to venturing onto this section.

I want - Quiero
I need - Necesito
I must - Debo
I have to - Tengo que
I have - Tengo
I can - Puedo
I like - Me gusta
I go - Yo voy / Me voy

I want to go to my house.
Yo quiero ir a mi casa.
I can go with you to the bus station.
Puedo ir contigo a la estación de autobuses.
I need to walk outside the museum.
Necesito caminar fuera del museo.
I like to eat oranges.
Me gusta comer naranjas.
I am going to teach a class.
Yo voy a enseñar una clase.

Please master *every* single page up until here prior to attempting the following pages!

You want / do you want? - Quieres / ¿Quieres?
He wants / does he want? - Quiere / ¿Quiere?
She wants / does she want? - Quiere / ¿Quiere?
We want / do we want? - Queremos / ¿Queremos?
They want / do they want? - Quieren / ¿Quieren?
You (plural) want? - Quieren / ¿Quieren?

You need / do you need? - Necesitas / ¿Necesitas?
He needs / does he need? - Necesita / ¿Necesita?
She needs / does she need? - Necesita / ¿Necesita?
We want / do we want? - Necesitamos / ¿Necesitamos?
They need / do they need? - Necesitan / ¿Necesitan?
You (plural) need? - Necesitan / ¿Necesitan?

You can / can you? - Puedes / ¿Puedes?
He can / can he? - Puede / ¿Puede?
She can / can she? - Puede / ¿Puede?
We can / can we? - Podemos / ¿Podemos?
They can / can they? - Pueden / ¿Pueden?
You (plural) can? - Pueden / ¿Pueden?

You like / do you like? - Te gusta / ¿Te gusta?
He likes / does he like? - Le gusta / ¿Le gusta?
She like / does she like? - Le gusta / ¿Le gusta?
We like / do we like? - Nos gusta / ¿Nos gusta?
They like / do they like? - Les gusta / ¿Les gusta?
You (plural) like? - Les gusta / ¿Les gusta?

You go / do you go? - Vas / ¿Vas?
He goes / does he go? - Va / ¿Va?
She goes / does she go? - Va / ¿Va?
We go / do we go? - Vamos / ¿Vamos?
They go / do they go? - Van / ¿Van?
You (plural) go? - Van / ¿Van?

You have / do you have? - Tienes / ¿Tienes?
He has / does he have? - Tiene / ¿Tiene?
She has / does she have? - Tiene / ¿Tiene?
We have / do we have? - Tenemos / ¿Tenemos?
They have / do they have? - Tienen / ¿Tienen?
You (plural) have? - Tienen / ¿Tienen?

Do you want to go?
¿Quieres ir?

Does he want to fly?
¿Él quiere volar?

We want to swim.
Queremos nadar

Do they want to run?
Quieren correr

Do you need to clean?
¿Necesitas limpiar?

She needs to sing a song
Necesita cantar una canción

We need to travel
Necesitamos viajar

They don't need to fight
No necesitan luchar

You (plural) need to save your money.
Necesitan ahorrar su dinero.

Can you hear me?
¿Puedes escucharme?

He can dance very well.
Puede bailar muy bien.

We can go out tonight.
Podemos salir esta noche.

The fireman can break the door during an emergency.
Los bomberos pueden romper la puerta durante una emergencia.

Do you like to eat here?
¿Te gusta comer aquí? / (formal) Le gusta a usted comer aquí?

He likes to spend time here.
Él gusta pasar tiempo aquí.

We like to stay in the house.
Nos gusta quedarnos en casa.

They like to cook.
Les gustan cocinar.

You (plural) like to play soccer.
Les gustan jugar fútbol.

Do you go to the movies on weekends?
¿Vas al cine en los fines de semana?

He goes fishing.
Él va a pescar.

We are going to relax.
Vamos a relajarnos.

They go out to eat at a restaurant everyday.
Todos los días salen a comer a un restaurante.

Do you have money?
¿Tienes dinero?

She has to look outside.
Ella tiene que mirar afuera.

We have to sign our names.
Tenemos que firmar nuestros nombres.

They have to send the letter.
Tienen que enviar la carta.

You (plural) have to wait in line.
Ustedes tienen que esperar en la línea.

Present Tense Indicative: Regular Verbs

In the Spanish language all infinitive forms of the verbs end in: "ar", "er", "ir".

The verbs are conjugated in the present tense of the indicative form by just adding the following personal endings to the stem of the verb.

	Hablar	Comer	Vivir
Yo	hablo	como	vivo
Tu	hablas	comes	vives
El, ella, usted	habla	come	vive
Nostro/as	hablamos	comemos	vivemos
Vosotros/as	hablais	comeis	vivis
Ellos, ellas, ustedes	hablan	comen	viven
AR VERBS	**ER VERBS**		**IR VERBS**

The asterisk* represents irregular verbs.

AR	ER	IR
Comprar - To buy	**Beber** - To drink	**Abrir** - To open
Bailar - To dance	**Comer** - To eat	**Escribir** - To write
Cambiar - To change	**To leer** - To read	**Assistir** - To assist
Desear - To wish	**Creer** - To believe	**Insistir** - To insist
Preguntar - To ask	**Responder** - To respond	**Recibir** - To receive
Trabajar - To work	**Vender** - To sell	***Preferir** - To prefer
Necesitar - To need	**Leer** - To read	***Incluir** - To include
Tomar - To take	***Querer** - To want	***Salir** - To leave
Llegar - To arrive	**Obedecer** - To obey	***Servir** - To serve
Ayudar - To help	***Tener** - To have	***Decir** - To say
Estudiar - To study	**Comprender** - To understand	***Sentir** - To feel
Escuchar - To hear	***Saber** - To know	
Viajar - To travel		
Demorar - To delay	**Terminar** - To finish	

Other Useful Tools in the Spanish Language

Days of the Week - Días de la semana
Sunday - Domingo
Monday - Lunes
Tuesday - Martes
Wednesday - Miércoles
Thursday - Jueves
Friday - Viernes
Saturday - Sábado

Seasons - Estaciones
Spring - Primavera / **Summer -** Verano
Autumn - Otoño / **Winter -** Invierno

Colors - Colores
Black - Negro
White - Blanco
Gray - Gris
Red - Rojo
Blue - Azul
Yellow - Amarillo
Green - Verde
Orange - Naranja
Purple - Purpura
Brown - Marrón

Numbers - Números
One - Uno
Two - Dos
Three - Tres
Four - Cuatro
Five - Cinco
Six - Seis
Seven - Siete
Eight - Ocho
Nine - Nueve
Ten - Diez

Cardinal Directions - Direcciones cardinales
North - Norte / **South -** Sur
East - Este / **West -** Oest

Conclusion

Congratulations! You have completed all the tools needed to master the Spanish language, and I hope that this has been a valuable learning experience. Now you have sufficient communication skills to be confident enough to embark on a visit to a Spanish-speaking county, impress your friends, and boost your resume so *good luck*.

This program is available in other languages as well, and it is my fervent hope that my language learning programs will be used for good, enabling people from all corners of the globe and from all cultures and religions to be able to communicate harmoniously. After memorizing the required three hundred and fifty words, please perform a daily five-minute exercise by creating sentences in your head using these words. This simple exercise will help you grasp conversational communications even more effectively. Also, once you memorize the vocabulary on each page, follow it by using a notecard to cover the words you have just memorized and test yourself and follow *that* by going back and using this same notecard technique on the pages you studied during the previous days. This repetition technique will assist you in mastering these words in order to provide you with the tools to create your own sentences.

Every day, use this notecard technique on the words that you have just studied.

Everything in life has a catch. The catch here is just consistency. If you just open the book, and after the first few pages of studying the program, you put it down, then you will not gain anything. However, if you consistently dedicate a half hour daily to studying, as well as reviewing what you have learned from previous days, then you will quickly realize why this method is the most effective technique ever created to become conversational in a foreign language. My technique works! For anyone who doubts this technique, all I can say is that it has worked for me and hundreds of others.

Conversational Spanish Quick and Easy
The Most Innovative Technique to Learn the Spanish Language

Part II

YATIR NITZANY

Translated by:
Semadar Mercedes Friedman

Interior Design:
Menachem Otto

Introduction to the Program

In the first book, you were taught the 350 most useful words in the Spanish language, which, once memorized, could be combined in order for you to create your own sentences. Now, with the knowledge you have gained, you can use those words in Conversational Spanish Quick and Easy Part 2 and Part 3, in order to supplement the 350 words that you've already memorized. This combination of words and sentences will help you master the language to even greater proficiency and quicker than with other courses.

The books that comprise Parts 2 and 3 have progressed from just vocabulary and are now split into various categories that are useful in our everyday lives. These categories range from travel to food to school and work, and other similarly broad subjects. In contrast to various other methods, the topics that are covered also contain parts of vocabulary that are not often broached, such as the military, politics, and religion. With these more unusual topics for learning conversational languages, the student can learn quicker and easier. This method is flawless and it has proven itself time and time again.

If you decide to travel to Spain or Latin America, then this book will help you speak the Spanish language.

This method has worked for me and thousands of others. It surpasses any other language-learning method system currently on the market today.

This book, Part 2, specifically deals with practical aspects concerning travel, camping, transportation, city living, entertainment such as films, food including vegetables and fruit, shopping, family including grandparents, in-laws, and stepchildren, human anatomy, health, emergencies, and natural disasters, and home situations.

The sentences within each category can help you get by in other countries.

In relation to travel, for example, you are given sentences about food, airport necessities such as immigration, and passports. Helpful phrases include, "Where is the immigration and passport control inside the airport?" and "I want to order a bowl of cereal and toast with jelly." For flights there are informative combinations such as, "There is a long line of passengers in the terminal because of the delay on the runway." When arriving in another country options for what to say include, "We

Introduction to the Program

want to hire a driver for the tour. However, we want to pay with a credit card instead of cash" and, "On which street is the car-rental agency?"

When discussing entertainment in another country and in a new language, you are provided with sentences and vocabulary that will help you interact with others. You can discuss art galleries and watching foreign films. For example, you may need to say to friends, "I need subtitles if I watch a foreign film" and, 'The mystery-suspense genre films are usually good movies'. You can talk about your own filming experience in front of the camera.

The selection of topics in this book is much wider than in ordinary courses. By including social issue such as incarceration, it will help you to engage with more people who speak the language you are learning.

Part 3 will deal with vocabulary and sentences relevant to indoor matters such as school and the office, but also a variety of professions and sports.

TRAVEL - VIAJE

Flight - Vuelo
Airplane - Avión
Airport – Aeropuerto / **Terminal** - Terminal
Passport - Pasaporte / **Customs** - Aduanas
Take off (airplane) – Despegar / **Landing** - Aterrizaje
Gate – Puerta de embarque / Embarque
Departure - Salida / **Arrival** – Llegada
Luggage - Equipaje / **Suitcase** - Maleta
Baggage claim - Recogida de equipaje
Passenger – **(Male)**Pasajero / **(Female)**pasajera
Final Destination – Destino final
Boarding - Embarque
Runway - Pista
Line - Línea
Delay - Demoro
Wing - Ala

I like to travel.
Me gusta viajar.
This is a very expensive flight.
Este es un vuelo muy caro (expensive).
The airplane takes off in the morning and lands at night.
El avión despega por la mañana y aterriza por la noche.
My suitcase is at the baggage claim.
Mi maleta está en la recogida de equipaje.
We need to go to the departure gate instead of the arrival gate.
Necesitamos ir a la puerta de salida en lugar de la puerta de llegada.
There is a long line of passengers in the terminal because of a delay on the runway.
Hay una larga línea de pasajeros en el terminal, por la demora en la pista.
What is your final destination?
¿Cuál es tu destino final?
I don't like to sit above the wing of the airplane.
No me gusta sentarme encima del la ala del avión.
The flight takes off at 3pm, but the boarding commences at 2:20pm.
El vuelo despega a las 3:00pm en punto., pero el embarque comienza a las 2:20pm.
Do I need to check in my luggage?
¿Tengo que registrar mi equipaje?
Where is the passport control inside the airport?
¿Dónde está el control de pasaportes en el aeropuerto?
I am almost finished at customs.
Casi termino con las aduanas.

Transportation

International flights – Vuelos internacionales
Domestic flights – Vuelos domésticos
First class – Primera clase
Business class – Clase ejecutiva
Economy class – Clase economía
Direct flight - Vuelo directo
Round trip - Viaje ida y vuelta
One-way flight - Vuelo de una dirección / **Return flight** - Vuelo de regreso
Flight attendant - Azafata /auxiliar de vuelo
Layover - Escala / **Connection** - Conexión
Reservation - Reservaciones / reservas
Security check – Control de seguridad
Checked bags - Maletas facturadas / **Carry-on bag** - Maleta de mano
Business trip - Viaje de negocios
Check in counter – Mostrador de facturación
Travel agency - Agencia de viajes
Temporary visa – Visa temporal / **Permanent visa** – Visa permanente
Country – País

The flight attendant told me to go to the check in counter.
La azafata me dijo que vaya al mostrador de facturación.
For international flights you must be at the airport at least three hours before the flight.
Para vuelos internacionales, debe de llegar al aeropuerto tres horas antes del vuelo.
For a domestic flight, I need to arrive at the airport at least two hours before the flight.
Para un vuelo doméstico, necesito llegar al aeropuerto al menos dos horas antes del vuelo.
Business class is usually cheaper than first class.
La clase ejecutiva en general (usually) es más barata (cheaper) que la primera clase.
Through the travel agency, the one-way ticket was cheaper than the round-trip ticket.
A través de la agencia de viajes, el boleto de una dirección era más barato que el boleto de ida y vuelta.
I prefer a direct flight without a layover.
Prefiero un vuelo directo sin escala.
I must make reservations for my return flight.
Tengo que reservar mi vuelo de regreso.
Why do I need to remove my shoes at the security check?
¿Por qué tengo que quitar mis zapatos en el control de seguridad?
I have three checked bags and one carry-on.
Tengo tres maletas facturadas y una de mano.
I have to ask my travel agent if this country requires a visa.
Tengo que preguntar a mi agente de viajes si este país requiere una visa.

Trip – Viaje
Tourist - Turista / **Tourism** - Turismo
Holidays - Fiestas / **Vacations** - Vacaciones
Currency exchange - Cambio de efectivo
Port of entry - Puerto de entrada
Car rental agency - Agencia de automóviles para alquilar
Identification - Identificación
GPS - GPS
Road - La carretera
Map - Mapa
Information center - Centro de Información
Bank - Banco
Hotel – Hotel / **Motel** - Motel / **Hostel** - Hostal
Leisure - Ocio / divertimiento
Driver – **(Male)** Conductor/ **(Female)** conductora
Tour - Excursión
Credit - Crédito / **Cash** - Efectivo
A guide - Un guía
Ski Resort - Estación de esquí

I had an amazing trip.
Tuve un viaje asombroso (amazing).
The currency exchange counter is past the port of entry.
El mostrador (counter) de cambio de efectivo esta al pasar de la entrada.
There is a lot of tourism during the holidays and vacations.
Hay mucho turismo durante las fiestas y las vacaciones.
Where is the car-rental agency?
¿Dónde está la agencia de automóviles para alquilar?
You need to show your identification whenever checking at a hotel
Tienes que mostrar tu identificación cada vez que tu te registras en un hotel.
It's more convenient to use the GPS on the roads instead of a map.
Usar el GPS es más conveniente que usar un mapa en las carreteras.
Why is the information center closed today?
¿Por qué el centro de información está cerrado hoy?
When I am in a new country, I go to the bank before I go to the hotel.
Cuando estoy en un nuevo país, voy al banco antes de llegar al hotel.
I need to book my leisure vacation at the ski resort today.
Necesito reservar mis vacaciones de ocio en el hotel de estación de esquí hoy.
We want to hire a driver for the tour.
Queremos contratar un conductor para el excursión.
We want to pay with a credit card instead of cash.
Queremos pagar con tarjeta de crédito en-lugar (in lieu of) de efectivo.
Does the tour include an English-speaking guide?
¿El recorrido incluye un guía que habla inglés?

TRANSPORTATION - TRANSPORTE

Car - Auto / automóvil / coche
Bus - Autobús
Station - Estación
Train - Tren **/ Train station -** Estación de tren
Train tracks - Vías del ferrocarril **/ Train cart -** Carro de tren
Subway - Subterráneo
Ticket - Boleto
Taxi - Taxi
Motorcycle – Motocicleta
Scooter - Scooter
Helicopter - Helicóptero
School bus – Autobús escolar
Limousine - Limusina
Driver license - Licencia de conducir
Vehicle registration - Registro de vehículos **/ License plate -** Plata de matrícula
Ticket (penalty) - Multa

Where is the public transportation?
¿Dónde está el transporte público?
Where can I buy a bus ticket?
¿Dónde puedo comprar un boleto de autobús?
Please call a taxi.
Por favor llame un taxi.
In some cities you don't need a car because you can rely on the subway.
En algunas ciudades no hace falta (there is no need) un automóvil, se cuenta con el metro.
Where is the train station?
¿Dónde está la estación de tren?
The train cart is still stuck on the tracks.
El carro del tren todavía está atascado (stuck) en las vías de ferrocarril.
The motorcycles make loud noises.
Las motocicletas hacen mucho ruido (noise).
Where can I rent a scooter?
¿Dónde puedo alquilar un scooter?
I want to schedule a helicopter tour.
Quiero programar un recorrido en helicóptero.
I want to go to the party in a limousine.
Quiero ir a la fiesta en una limusina.
Don't forget to bring your driver's license and registration.
No olvides de traer tu licencia de conducir y registro del vehículo.
The cop gave me a ticket because my license plate is expired.
La policía me dio una multa porque mi placa de matrícula estaba expirada.

Truck – Camión / **Pickup truck** - Camioneta
Bicycle – Bicicleta
Van - Camioneta
Gas station – Gasolinera
Gasoline - Gasolina
Tire - Llanta
Oil change – Cambio de aceite
Tire change – Cambio de llanta
Mechanic – Mecánico
Canoe - Canoa
Ship / Boat – Barco
Yacht - Yate
Sailboat - Velero / **Motorboat** – Motora
Marina - Marina
A dock - Un muelle
Cruise / cruise ship - Crucero
Ferry - Ferry
Submarine – Submarino

I have to put my bicycle in my truck.
Pongo mis bicycleta en mi camion.
Where is the gas station?
¿Donde está la gasolinera?
I need gasoline and also to put air in my tires.
Tengo que llenar gasolina y poner aire en mis llantas.
I need to take my car to the mechanic for a tire and oil change.
Necesito llevar mi automóvil al mecánico para un cambio de llantas y un cambio de aceite.
I can bring my canoe in the van.
Puedo traer mi canoa en mi camioneta.
Can I bring my yacht to the boat show at the marina?
¿Puedo llevar mi yate a la exhibición de barcos en la marina?
I prefer a motorboat instead of a sailboat.
Prefiero un bote a motor en-vez (instead) de un velero.
I want to leave my boat at the dock on the island.
Quiero dejar mi bote en el muelle de la isla.
This spot is a popular stopping point for the cruise ship.
Este lugar es un punto de parada popular para el crucero.
This was an incredible cruise.
Este era un crucero increíble.
Do you have the schedule for the ferry?
¿Tienes el horario (the schedule) para el ferry?
The submarine is yellow.
El submarino es amarillo

CITY - CIUDAD

Town / village - Pueblo
House – Casa / **Home -** Hogar
Apartment - Apartamento
Tower - Torre
Building - Edificio / inmueble
Skyscraper – Rascacielos
Neighborhood – Barrio
Office building – Edificio de oficinas
Location - Ubicación
Elevator – Ascensor
Stairs - Escaleras
Fence - Cerca
Construction site – Sitio de construcción
Post office – Oficina de correo
Bridge - Puente
Gate - Puerta
City hall – Alcaldía / **The mayor -** El alcalde, (f) la alcaldesa
Fire department – Departamento de bomberos

Is this a city or a village?
¿Es esta una ciudad o un pueblo?
Does he live in a house or an apartment?
¿Vive en una casa o en un apartamento?
This residential building does not have an elevator, just stairs.
El inmueble residencial no tiene ascensor, solo escaleras.
These skyscrapers are located in the new part of the city.
Estos rascacielos se encuentran (can be found) en la parte nueva de la ciudad.
The tower is tall but the building beside it is very short.
La torre es alta pero el edificio al lado es muy bajo.
This is a historical neighborhood.
Este es un barrio histórico.
There is a fence around the construction site.
Hay una cerca alrededor del sitio de construcción.
The post office is located in that office building.
La oficina de correo se encuentra en ese edificio de oficinas.
The bridge is closed today.
El puente está cerrado hoy
The gate is open.
La puerta está abierta.
The fire department is located in the building next to city hall.
El departamento de bomberos está ubicado (located) en el edificio al lado de la alcaldía.

Street - La calle / **Main street** - Calle principal
Parking / parking lot - Estacionamiento
Sidewalk - La acera
Traffic - Tráfico
Traffic light - Semáforo
Red light – La luz roja / **Yellow light** - La luz amarilla
Green light – La luz verde
Toll lane - Carril de peaje / **Fast lane** – Carril rápido / **Slow lane** – Carril lento
Left lane – Carril izquierdo / **Right lane** – Carril derecho
Highway – Autopista, carretera / **Intersection** - Intersección / **Tunnel** – Túnel
U-turn - Cambio de sentido / **Shortcut** - Atajo
Stop sign - Señal de stop / **Pedestrians** - Peatones / **Crosswalk** - Paso de peatones

The parking is on the main street and not on the sidewalk.
El estacionamiento está en la calle principal y no en la acera.
Where is the parking lot?
¿Dónde está el estacionamiento?
The traffic is very bad today.
El tráfico es muy malo (bad) hoy.
You must avoid the fast lane because it's a toll lane.
Debe evitar el carril rápido porque es un carril de peaje.
I hate to drive on the highway.
Odio manejar en la autopista.
At a red light you need to stop, at a yellow light you must be prepared to stop and at a green you can drive.
En una luz roja, debe detenerse, en una luz amarilla debe prepararse para detenerse, y en una luz verde puedes manejar.
I don't like traffic lights.
No me gustan los semáfaros.
At the intersection, you need to stay in the right lane instead of the left lane because that's a bus lane.
En la intersección, debe permanecer en el carril derecho en lugar del carril izquierdo porque es un carril del autobús.
The tunnel is very long, however, it seems short.
El túnel es muy largo (long), sin embargo, parece (seems) corto (short).
It's a long way.
Es un camino largo.
The next bus stop is far.
La próxima parada del autobús es lejos.
You need to turn right at the stop sign and then continue on straight.
Debe girar a la derecha en la señal de stop y luego continuar derecho.
Pedestrians use the crosswalk to cross the road.
Los peatones usan el paso de peatones para cruzar la calle.

City

Capital – La capital
Resort - Recurso
Port - Puerto
Road - La carretera / camino
Trail – Sendero
Bus station - Estación de autobuses
Bus stop – Parada de autobús
Night club – Club nocturno
Downtown – Centro de la ciudad
District - Distrito
County - Condado
Statue - Estatua
Monument - Monumento
Castle – Castillo
Cathedral - Catedral
Zoo – Parque zoológico
Science museum – Museo de Ciencia
Playground – Campo de recreo
Swimming pool – Piscina
Jail – Cárcel / **Prison** – Prisión

The capital is a major attraction point for tourists.
La capital es un importante punto de atracción para los turistas.
The resort is next to the port.
El recurso está al lado del puerto.
The night club is located in the downtown district.
El club nocturno está en el centro de la ciudad.
This statue is a monument to the city.
Esta estatua es un monumento de la ciudad.
This is an ancient castle.
Este es un castillo antiguo.
That is a beautiful cathedral.
Esta es una linda catedral.
Do you want to go to the zoo or the science museum?
¿Quieres ir al parque zoológico o al museo de ciencias?
The children are in the playground.
Los niños están en el campo de recreo.
The swimming pool is closed for the community today.
Hoy la piscina está cerrada para la comunidad.
You need to follow the trail alongside the main street to reach the bus station.
Tienes que seguir el sendero junto a la calle principal para llegar a la estación de autobuses.
There is a jail in this county, but not a prison.
Hay una cárcel en este condado, sin embargo (however), no hay el prisión.

ENTERTAINMENT - ENTRETENIMIENTO

Movie / film - Película
Theater (movie theater) - Cine
Actor – Actor **/ Actress -** Actriz
Genre – Género
Subtitles – Subtítulos
Action - Acción
Foreign - Extranjero
Mystery – Misterio
Suspense – Suspenso
Documentary - Documentaría **/ Biography -** Biografía
Drama - Drama
Comedy - Comedia
Romance - Romance
Horror – Horror
Animation - Animación
Cartoon – Dibujos animados
Director – Director **/ Producer -** Productor **/ Audience –** Audiencia, publico

There are three new movies at the theater that I want to see.
Hay tres nuevas películas en el cine que quiero ver.
He is a really good actor.
Él es un muy buen actor.
She is an excellent actress
Ella es una excelente actriz.
That was a good action movie
Esa fue una buena película de acción
I need subtitles when I watch a foreign film
Necesito subtítulos si veo una película extranjera.
Films of the mystery-suspense genre are usually good movies.
Las películas de género de suspenso misterioso suelen ser buenas películas.
I like documentary films. However, comedy-drama or romance films are better.
Me gustan las películas de documentarios. Aunque (although), las comedias dramáticas o románticas son superiores.
My favorite genre of movies are the horror movies.
Mi género favorito de películas es el horror.
It's fun to watch cartoons and animated movies.
Es divertido (fun) ver dibujos animados y películas animadas.
Sometimes biographies are boring to watch.
A veces las biografías son aburridas de ver.
The director and the producer can meet the audience today.
El director y el productor pueden ver a la audiencia hoy.

Entertainment - Entretenimiento
Television - Televisión (program)
Television - Televisor (actual device)
A show - Programa (as in television)
A show - Un espectáculo (as in live perfromance)
Channel – Canal
Series - Serie
Commercial - Comercial
Episode - Episodio
Anchorman - Presentador
Anchorwoman - Presentadora
News - Noticias
News station – Noticiero / estación de noticias
Screening - Proyección
Live - En vivo / en directo
Broadcast - Emisión / transmisión
Headline - Título
Viewer – Espectador
Speech – Discurso
Script - Guión
Screen - Pantalla
Camera - Cámara

It's time to buy a new television.
Es hora de comprar un nuevo televisor.
This was the first episode of this television show yet it was a long series.
Este fue el primer episodio de este programa de televisión pero era una larga seria.
There aren't any commercials on this channel.
En este canal, no hay comerciales.
This anchorman and anchorwoman work for our local news station.
Estos presentador y presentadora trabajan para nuestra estación de noticias locales.
They decided to screen a live broadcast on the news.
Decidieron proyectar una transmisión en vivo en las noticias.
The news station featured the headlines before the program began.
La estación de noticias presento los titulares antes de que comenzara el programa.
Tonight, all the details about the incident were mentioned on the news.
Esta noche, todos los detalles sobre el incidente fueron mencionados en las noticias.
The viewers wanted to hear the presidential speech today.
Los espectadores querían escuchar el discurso del presidente hoy.
I must read my script in front of the screen and the camera
Tengo que leer mi guión delante de la pantalla y la cámara.
We want to enjoy the entertainment tonight.
Queremos disfrutar del entretenimiento esta noche.

Entertainment

Theater (play) – Teatro
A musical - Un musical
A play - Una obra
Stage – Escenario
Audition - Audición
Performance – Actuación
Box office – Taquilla, taquillera / **Ticket** – Boleto, entrada
Singer – Cantante / **Band** – Grupo
Orchestra - Orquesta
Opera - Ópera
Music - Música
Song - Canción
Musical instrument – Instrumento musical
Drum - Tambor
Guitar - Guitarra
Piano - Piano
Trumpet – Trompeta
Violin – Violín
Flute - Flauta
Art - Arte
Gallery - Galería
Studio - Estudio
Museum – Museo

It was a great musical performance.
Fue una gran actuación musical.
Can I audition for the play on this stage?
¿Puedo hacer una audición para la obra en este escenario?
She is the lead singer of the band.
Ella es la cantante principal (main) del grupo.
I will go to the box office tomorrow to purchase tickets for the opera.
Mañana iré a la taquilla a comprar entradas para la ópera.
The orchestra needs to perform below the stage.
La orquesta necesita actuar de bajo del escenario.
I like to listen to this type of music. I hope to hear a good song.
Me gusta escuchar este tipo de música. Espero escuchar una buena canción.
The most popular musical instruments that are used in a concert are drums, guitars, pianos, trumpets, violins, and flutes.
En un concierto los instrumentos musicales más popular que se usan son tambores, guitarras, pianos, trompetas, violines, y flautas.
The art gallery has a studio for rent.
La galería de arte tiene un estudio para alquilarlo.
I went to an art museum yesterday.
Fui a un museo de arte ayer.

FOODS - COMIDAS / ALIMENTACIÓN

Grocery store - Tienda de comestibles / **Market** - Mercado
Supermarket - Supermercado
Groceries - Comestibles
Butcher shop - Carnicería / **Butcher** - Carnicero
Bakery - Panadería / **Baker** - Panadero
Breakfast – Desayunó / **Lunch** – Almuerzo / **Dinner** – Cena
Meat - Carne / **Chicken** - Pollo
Seafood – Mariscos
Milk - Leche/ **Cheese** - Queso / **Butter** – Mantequilla
Egg – Huevo / **Oil** - Aceite / **Flour** - Harina
Bread - Pan
Baked - Horneado
Cake - Pastel
Beer - Cerveza / **Wine** – Vino
Cinnamon - Canela
Powder - Polvo
Mustard - Mostaza

Where is the nearest grocery store?
¿Dónde está la más cerca tienda de comestibles?
Where can I buy meat and chicken?
¿Dónde puedo comprar carne y pollo?
I need to buy flour, eggs, milk, butter, and oil to bake my cake.
Necesito comprar harina, huevos, leche, mantequilla y aceite para hornear mi pastel.
The groceries are already in the car.
Los comestibles ya están en el auto.
It's easy to find papayas and coconuts at the supermarket.
Es fácil encontrar papayas y cocos en el supermercado.
Where can I buy beer and wine.
Donde puedo comprar cerveza y vino.
On which aisle is the cinnamon powder?
¿En qué pasillo (aisle) está el polvo de canela?
The butcher shop is near the bakery.
La carnicería esta al lado de la panadería.
I have to go to the market, to buy a half pound of meat.
Tengo que ir al mercado, para comprar media (half) libra (pound) de carne.
For lunch, we can eat seafood, and then pasta for dinner.
Para el almuerzo, podemos comer mariscos y luego pasta para la cena.
I usually eat bread with cheese for breakfast.
Normalmente como pan con queso para el desayuno.
I don't have any ketchup or mustard to put on my hotdog.
No tengo ketchup o mostaza para poner en mí salchicha.

Menu - Menú
Beef - Carne de vaca / **Lamb -** Cordero / **Pork -** Cerdo
Steak - Filete/bistec
Hamburger - Hamburguesa
Water – Agua
Salad - Ensalada
Soup - Sopa
Appetizer – Aperitivo / **Entrée –** Entrada
Cooked - Cocido
Boiled - Hervido / **Fried -** Frito / **Grilled -** A la parrilla, asado
Raw - Crudo
Coffee – Café
Dessert – Postre
Ice cream - Helado
Olive oil – Aceite de oliva
Fish – Pescado
Juice - Jugo
Tea – Té
Honey – Miel / **Sugar -** Azúcar

Do you have a menu in English?
¿Tiene usted un menú en inglés?
Which is preferable, the fried pork or the grilled lamb?
¿Cuál es preferible, el cerdo frito o el cordero a la parrilla?
I want to order a cup of water, a soup for my appetizer, and pizza for my entrée.
Quiero pedir un vaso de agua, una sopa para mi aperitivo, y una pizza para mi plato principal.
I want to order a steak for myself, a hamburger for my son, and ice cream for my wife.
Quiero ordenar un filete para mí, una hamburguesa para mi hijo, y un helado para mi esposa.
Which type of dessert is included with my coffee?
¿Qué tipo de postre está incluido con mi café?
Can I order a salad with a boiled egg and olive oil on the side?
¿Puedo pedir una ensalada con un huevo cocido y aceite de oliva de lado?
This fish isn't well cooked, it is still raw inside.
Este pescado, no está bien cocido, todavía está crudo.
I want to order a fruit juice instead of a soda.
Quiero ordenar un jugo de frutas en vez de una soda.
I want to order tea with a teaspoon of honey instead of sugar.
Quiero ordenar un té con una cucharadita de miel en lugar de azúcar.
The tip is 20% at this restaurant.
La propina (tip) en este restaurante es 20 por-ciento (percent).

Foods

Vegetarian - Vegetariano
Vegan – Vegano
Dairy products - Lácteos / productos de leche
Salt - Sal
Pepper - Pimienta
Flavor - Sabor
Spices - Especias
Rice - Arroz / **Fries -** Papas fritas
Soy - Soja
Nuts - Nueces
Peanuts - Cacahuetes/ maní
Sauce - Salsa
Sandwich - Bocadillo
Mayonnaise - Mayonesa
Jelly - Mermelada
Chocolate - Chocolate / **Cookie -** Galleta, bizcocho / **Candy -** Dulces
Whipped cream - Crema batida
Popsicle - Paleta
Frozen - Congelado / **Thawed –** Descongelado

I don't eat meat because I am a vegetarian.
No como carne porque soy vegetariano.
My brother won't eat dairy because he is a vegan.
Mi hermano no come lácteos porque él es un vegano.
Food tastes much better with salt, pepper, and spices.
La comida tiene mejor sabor con sal, pimienta, y especias.
The only things I have in my freezer are popsicles.
Lo único que tengo en mi congeladora son paletas heladas.
No chocolate, candy, or whipped cream until after dinner.
No chocolate, ni dulces, o crema batida hasta después de la cena.
I want to try a sample of that piece of cheese.
Quiero probar una muestra (sample) de ese trozo (slice/piece) de queso.
I have allergies to nuts and peanuts.
Tengo alergias a las nueces y al maní.
This sauce is disgusting.
Esta salsa es asquerosa.
Why do you always put mayonnaise on your sandwich?
¿Por qué siempre pones mayonesa en tu bocadillo?
The food is still frozen so we need to wait for it to thaw.
La comida todavía está congelada, por eso debemos esperar a que se descongele.
Please bring me a bowl of cereal and a slice of toasted bread with jelly.
Por favor dame un tazón de cereal y una rebanada de pan tostado con mermelada.
It's healthier to eat rice instead of fries.
Es más saludable comer arroz que papas fritas.

VEGETABLES - VERDURAS / VEGETALES

Grilled vegetables – Vegetales asados / **Steamed vegetables** – Verduras al vapor
Tomato – Tomate / **Carrot** – Zanahoria / **Lettuce** - Lechuga
Radish - Rábano
Beet - Remolacha
Eggplant - Berenjena
Bell Pepper – Pimiento / **Hot pepper** – Ají picante
Celery - Apio
Spinach - Espinacas
Cabbage - Col / **Cauliflower** - Coliflor
Beans – Frijoles
Corn - Maíz
Garlic - Ajo / **Onion** - Cebolla
Artichoke - Alcachofa

Grilled vegetables or steamed vegetables are popular side dishes at restaurants.
Las verduras a la parrilla o las verduras al vapor son platos populares en los restaurantes.
I put carrots, bell peppers, lettuce, and radishes in my salad.
Yo pongo zanahorias, pimientos, lechuga, y rábanos en mi ensalada.
It's not hard to grow tomatoes.
No es difícil cultivar tomates.
Eggplant can be cooked or fried.
La berenjena se puede cocinar o freír.
I like to put beets in my salad.
Me gusta poner remolachas en la ensalada.
Why are chili peppers so spicy?
¿Por qué estos chili pimientos son tan picantes?
Celery and spinach have natural vitamins.
El apio y la espinaca tienen vitaminas naturales.
Fried cauliflower tastes better than fried cabbage.
Coliflor frito es más agradable que col frito.
Rice and beans are my favorite side dish.
El arroz y los frijoles son mi plato favorito
I like to put butter on corn
Me gusta poner mantequilla al maíz.
Garlic is an important ingredient in many cuisines.
El ajo es un ingrediente importante en muchas cocinas.
Where is the onion powder?
¿Dónde está el polvo de cebolla?
Artichokes are difficult to peel.
Las alcachofas son difíciles de pelar.

Cucumber – Pepino
Lentil – Lenteja / **Peas** - Guisante / chícharos
Green onion – Cebolla verde
Herbs - Hierbas
Parsley - Perejil / **Cilantro** - Cilantro
Basil - Albahaca / **Dill** – Eneldo / **Mint** - Yerba buena
Potatoes – Papas / patatas / **Sweet Potato** - Batata
Mushroom – Hongo
Asparagus - Espárragos
Seaweed – Algas marinas
Pumpkin – Calabaza / **Squash** - Calabaza / **Zucchini** - Calabacín
Chick peas – Garbanzos
Vegetable garden – Huerto / jardín de vegetales

I want to order lentil soup.
Quiero ordenar sopa de lentejas.
Please put the green onion in the refrigerator.
Por favor ponga las cebollitas verdes en el refrigerador.
The most common kitchen herbs are basil, cilantro, dill, parsley, and mint.
Las hierbas más comunes en la cocina son la albahaca, el cilantro, el eneldo, el perejil, y la yerba buena.
Some of the most common vegetables for tempura are sweet potatoes and mushrooms.
Algunas verduras de las más comunes para tempura son las batatas y los hongos.
I want to order vegetarian sushi with asparagus and cucumber, along with a side of seaweed salad.
Quiero pedir sushi vegetariano con espárragos y pepino y una adición de ensalada de algas.
I enjoy eating pumpkin seeds as a snack.
Disfruto comer semillas (seeds) de calabaza como merienda.
I need to water my vegetable garden.
Necesito regar mi huerto.
The potatoes in the field are ready to harvest.
Las papas en el campo (field) están listas para cosecharlas.
Chickpeas are the main ingredient to make hummus.
Los garbanzos son el ingrediente principal para hacer humus.
Zucchini and squash are from the same family of vegetables.
El calabacín y la calabaza son de la misma familia de verduras.
Pickled ginger is extremely healthy for you.
El jengibre en escabeche es extremadamente saludable (healthy) para ti.
The tomatoes are fresh but the cucumbers are rotten.
Los tomates son frescos (fresh) pero los pepinos están podridos (rotten).

FRUITS - FRUTAS

Apple - Manzana / **Banana -** Banana / **Peach -** Durazno
Orange - Naranja / **Grapefruit -** Toronja
Tropical fruit - Fruta tropical
Papaya - Papaya
Coconut - Coco
Cherry - Cereza
Raisin - Pasa / **Prune -** Ciruela la seca
Dates - Dátiles
Fig - Higo
Fruit salad - Ensalada de frutas
Dried fruit - Fruta seca
Apricot - Albaricoque
Pear - Pera
Avocado - Aguacate
Ripe - Maduro

Can I add raisins to the apple pie?
¿Puedo agregar pasas a la tarta (pie) de manzana?
Orange juice is a wonderful source of Vitamin C.
El jugo de naranja es una maravillosa fuente (source) de vitamina C.
Grapefruits are extremely beneficial for your health.
Las toronjas son extremadamente beneficiosas para su salud (health).
I have a peach tree in my front yard.
Tengo un árbol de durazno en mi jardin.
It's easy to find papayas and coconuts at the supermarket.
Es fácil encontrar papayas y cocos en el supermercado.
I want to travel to Japan to see the famous cherry blossom.
Quiero viajar al Japón para ver la famosa flor de cerezas.
Bananas are tropical fruits.
Las bananas son frutas tropicales.
I want to mix dates and figs in my fruit salad.
Quiero mezclar dátiles e higos en mi ensalada de frutas.
Apricots and prunes are my favorite dried fruits.
Los albaricoques y las ciruelas son mis frutas secas (dried) favoritas.
Pears are delicious.
Las peras son deliciosas.
The avocados aren't ripe yet.
Los aguacates aún no están maduros (ripe).
The green apple is very sour.
La manzana verde es muy agria (sour).
The unripe peach is usually bitter.
El durazno inmaduro (unripe) suele (usually) ser amargo (bitter).

Fruit tree - Árbol de frutas
Citrus - Cítricos
Lemon - Limón
Lime - Lima
Pineapple - Piña
Melon - Melón
Watermelon - Sandía
Strawberry - Fresa
Berry - Baya / moras
Raspberry – Frambuesa / **Blueberry** - Arándano
Grape - Uva
Pomegranate - Granada
Plum - Ciruela
Olive - Aceituna
Grove - Arboleda

Strawberries grow during the Spring.
Las fresas crecen durante la primavera.
How much does the watermelon juice cost?
¿Cuánto cuesta el jugo de sandía?
I have a pineapple plant inside a pot.
Tengo una planta de piña en una maceta (plant pot).
Melons grow on the ground.
Los melones crecen en la tierra (ground).
I am going to the fruit-tree section of the nursery today to purchase a few citrus trees.
Hoy voy a la sección de árboles frutales del vivero (nursery) para comprar algunos cítricos.
There are many raspberries on the bush.
Hay muchas frambuesas en el arbusto (bush).
Blueberry juice is very sweet.
El jugo de arándano es muy dulce.
Berriess are acidic fruits.
Las bayas son frutas ácidas.
Pomegranate juice contains a very high level of antioxidants.
El jugo de la granada contiene un nivel (level) muy alto de antioxidantes.
I need to pick the grapes to make the wine.
Necesito recoger las uvas para hacer el vino.
Plums are seasonal fruits.
Las ciruelas son frutas temporadas (seasonal).
I must add either lemon juice or lime juice to my salad
Debo agregar jugo de limón o jugo de lima en mi ensalada.
I have an olive grove in my backyard.
Tengo un olivar en mí jardín.

SHOPPING - COMPRAS

Clothes - Ropa
Clothing store - Tienda de ropa
For sale - Se vende / en venta
Hat - Sombrero
Shirt - Camisa
Shoes - Zapatos
Skirt - Falda / **Dress** - Vestido
Pants - Pantalones / **Shorts** - Pantalones cortos
Suit - Traje / **Vest** - Chaleco / **Tie** - Corbata
Uniform - Uniforme
Belt - Cinturón
Socks - Calcetines
Gloves - Guantes
Glasses - Lentes / **Sunglasses** - Gafas
Size - Talla / tamaño
Small - Pequeño, **(f)** pequeña
Medium - Medio
Large - Grande
Thin - Delgado, **(f)** delgada / **Thick** - Grueso, **(f)** gruesa
Thrift store - Tienda de segunda mano

There are a lot of clothes for sale today.
Hoy hay mucha ropa que se vende.
Does this hat look good?
¿Se ve bien este sombrero?
I am happy with this shirt and these shoes.
Estoy contento con esta camisa y estos zapatos.
She prefers a skirt instead of a dress.
Ella prefiere una falda en vez de un vestido.
These pants aren't my size.
Estos pantalones no son de mi talla.
Where can I find a thrift store? I want to buy a suit, a vest, and a tie.
¿Dónde puedo encontrar una tienda de segunda mano? Quiero comprar un traje, un chaleco, y una corbata.
There are uniforms for school at the clothing store.
Hay uniformes para la escuela en la tienda de ropa.
I forgot my socks, belt, and shorts at your house.
Olvidé mis calcetines, cinturón y pantalones cortos en tu casa.
These gloves are a size too small. Do you have a medium size?
Estos guantes son de una talla demasiado pequeña. ¿Tienes una talla mediana?
Today I don't need my reading glasses. I only need my sunglasses.
No necesito mis lentes para leer hoy. Solo necesito mis gafas.

Jacket - Chaqueta
Scarf - Bufanda
Mittens - Guantes
Sleeve - Mangas
Boots (rain, winter) - Botas
Sweater - Suéter
Bathing suit - Traje de baño/bañador
Flip flops – Chanclas, chancletas / **Sandals -** Sandalias
Tank top - Camiseta
Heels - Tacones
On sale - En venta
Expensive - Costoso / caro
Free - Gratis
Discount – Descuento / **Cheap -** Barato
Shopping - Compras
Mall - Centro comercial

We are going to the mountain today so don't forget your jacket, mittens, and scarf.
Hoy vamos a la montaña que no te olvides tu chaqueta, los guantes y la bufanda.
I have long sleeve shirts and short sleeve shirts.
Tengo camisas de mangas largas y de mangas cortas.
Boots and sweaters are meant for winter.
Botas y suéter se usan en el invierno (winter).
At the beach, I wear a bathing suit and flip flops.
En la playa (beach) voy con un bañador y chanclas.
I want to buy a tank top for summer.
Quiero comprar una camiseta para el verano (summer).
I can't wear heels on the beach, only sandals.
No puedo usar tacones en la playa, solo sandalias.
What's on sale today?
¿Qué está en venta hoy?
This is free.
Esto es gratis.
Even though this cologne and this perfume are discounted, they are still very expensive.
A pesar de que este colone y este perfume tienen descuentos, todavía estan muy caros.
These items are very cheap.
Estos artículos son muy baratos.
I can go shopping only on weekends.
Puedo ir de compras solamente en fin-de-semanas (weekend).
Is the local mall far?
¿Está lejos el centro comercial local?

Shopping

Business hours - Horas de trabajo
Store - Tienda
Business hours - Horas de trabajo / horario de trabajo
Open - Abierto / **Closed** - Cerrado
Entrance - Entrada / **Exit** - Salida
Shopping cart - Carrito de compras / **Shopping basket** - Cesta de compras
Shopping bag - Bolsa de la compra
Toy store - Tienda de juguetes / **Toy** - Juguete
Book store – Librería/ **Music store** - Tienda de música
Jeweler - Joyero / **Jewelry** - Joyería / **Gold** - Oro / **Silver** - Plata
Necklace - Collar / **Bracelet** - Pulsera /
Earrings - Pendientes / **Diamond** - Diamante
Gift - Regalo
Coin – Moneda **Antique** - Antiguo / **Dealer** - Comerciante

What are your business hours?
¿Cuál es su horario de trabajo?
What time does the store open?
¿A qué hora abre la tienda?
What time does the store close?
¿A qué hora se cierra la tienda?
Where is the entrance?
¿Donde está la entrada?
Where is the exit?
¿Donde está la salida?
My children want to go to the toy store so that they can fill up the shopping cart with toys.
Mis hijos quieren ir a la juguetera para rellenar el carrito con muchos juguetes.
I need a large shopping basket when I go to the supermarket.
Necesito una gran cesta de compras cuando voy al supermercado.
Bookstores are almost non-existent since today everything that's for sale is online.
Las librerías casi no existen ya que hoy todo lo que está en venta, se vende por online.
It's difficult to find a music store these days.
Es difícil encontrar una tienda de música en estos días.
The jeweler sells gold and silver.
El joyero vende oro y plata.
I want to buy a diamond necklace.
Quiero comprar un collar de diamantes.
This bracelet and those pair of earrings are gifts for my daughter.
Esta pulsera y esos pendientes son regalos para mi hija.
He is an antique coin dealer.
Él es un comerciante de monedas antiguas.

FAMILY - FAMILIA

Mother - Madre
Father - Padre
Son - Hijo
Daughter - Hija
Brother - Hermano
Sister - Hermana
Husband - Marido / esposo
Wife - Esposa / mujer
Parents - Padres
Child - Niño / niña
Baby - Bebé
Grandparents - Abuelos
Grandfather - Abuelo
Grandmother - Abuela
Grandson - Nieto
Granddaughter - Nieta
Grandchildren - Nietos
Nephew - Sobrino **/ Niece -** Sobrina
Cousin - Primo /prima

I have a big family.
Tengo una gran familia.
My brother and sister are here.
Mi hermano y mi hermana están aquí.
The mother and father want to spend time with their child.
La madre y el padre quieren pasar-tiempo (to spend time) con su hijo.
He wants to bring his son and daughter.
Quiere traer a su hijo e hija.
The grandfather wants to take his grandson to the movie.
El abuelo quiere llevar a su nieto al cine.
The grandmother needs to give her granddaughter money.
La abuela necesita dar dinero (money) a su nieta.
The grandparents want to spend time with their grandchildren.
Los abuelos quieren pasar el tiempo con sus nietos.
The husband and wife have a new baby.
El esposo y la esposa tienen un nuevo bebé.
I want to go to the park with my niece and nephew.
Quiero ir al parque (park) con mi sobrina y sobrino.
My cousin wants to see his children.
Mi primo quiere ver a sus hijos.
That man is a good parent.
Ese hombre es un buen padre.

Aunt - Tía / **Uncle** - Tío
Man - Hombre / **Woman** - Mujer
Stepfather - Padrastro / **Stepmother** - Madrastra
Stepbrother - Hermanastro / **Stepsister** - Hermanastra
Stepson - Hijastro / **Stepdaughter** - Hijastra
Half-brother - Medio hermano / **Half-sister** - Media hermana
In laws - Suegros
Ancestor - Antepasado / **Family tree** - Árbol genealógico
Generation - Generación
First born - Primogénito / **Only child** - Hijo único
Relatives - Parientes / **Family members** - Familares, miembros de la familia
Twins - Gemelos
Pregnant - Embarazada
Adult - Adulto
Neighbor - Vecino, vecina / **Friend** - Amigo, amiga
Roommate - Compañero de cuarto
Adopted child - Niño adoptado / **Orphan** – Huérfano

My aunt and uncle are here for a visit.
Mi tía y mi tío me visitan.
He is their only child.
Él es su hijo único.
My wife is pregnant with twins.
Mi esposa está embarazada y son gemelos.
He is their eldest son.
Él es el primogénito.
The first-born child usually takes on all the responsibilities.
El primogénito generalmente asume todas las responsabilidades.
I was able to find all my relatives and ancestors on my family tree.
En mi árbol genealógico encontré a mis parientes y mis antepasados.
My parents' generation loved disco music.
La generación de mis padres amaban la música disco.
Their adopted child was an orphan
Él hijo adoptivo era un huérfano.
I like my in-laws.
Me gustan mis suegros.
I have a nice neighbor.
Tengo un buen vecino
We need to choose a godfather for his daughter.
Necesitamos elegir un padrino para su hija.
She considers her stepson as her real son.
Ella considera a su hijastro como su verdadero hijo.
She is his stepdaughter.
Ella es su hijastra.

HUMAN BODY - CUERPO HUMANO

Head - Cabeza
Face - Cara
Eye - Ojo / **Nose -** Nariz
Ear - Oreja
Mouth - Boca / **Lips -** Labios
Tongue - Lengua
Cheek - Mejilla
Chin - Mentón
Neck - Cuello / **Throat -** Garganta
Forehead - Frente / **Eyebrow -** Ceja / **Eyelashes -** Pestañas
Hair - Cabello / pelo
Beard - Barba / **Mustache -** Bigotes
Tooth - Diente

My chin, cheeks, mouth, lips, and eyes are all part of my face.
Mi mentón, mejillas, boca, labios y ojos son parte de mi cara.
He has small ears.
Él tiene orejas pequeñas.
I have a cold so my nose, eyes, mouth, and tongue are affected.
Tengo un resfriado que afectan mi nariz, ojos, boca y lengua.
The five senses are sight, touch, taste, smell, and hearing.
La vista, el tacto, el gusto, el olfato y el oído son los cinco sentidos.
I am washing my face right now.
Me estoy lavando la cara ahora mismo.
I have a headache
Tengo un dolor de cabeza.
My eyebrows are too long.
Mis cejas son demasiado largas.
He must shave his beard and mustache.
Debe afeitarse la barba y los bigotes.
I want to brush my teeth in the morning.
Quiero cepillar los dientes por la mañana.
She puts a lot of makeup on her cheeks and a lot of lipstick on her lips.
Tiene mucho maquillaje en sus mejillas y mucho pinte de labios.
Her hair covered her forehead.
Su cabello cubría su frente.
My hair is very long.
Mi pelo es muy largo.
She has a long neck.
Ella tiene un cuello largo.
I have a sore throat.
Tengo un dolor de garganta.

Shoulder - Hombro
Chest - Pecho
Arm - Brazo / **Elbow** - Codo / **Wrist** - Muñeca
Hand - Mano / **Palm** (of hand) - Palma
Finger - Dedo
Thumb - Pulgar
Back - Espalda
Brain - Cerebro / **Lungs** - Pulmones / **Heart** - Corazón / **Kidneys** - Riñones
Liver - Hígado / **Stomach** - Estómago / **Intestines** - Intestinos
Leg - Pierna / **Ankle** - Tobillo
Foot - Pie
Toe - Dedo del pie
Nail - Uña
Joint - Articulación
Muscle - Músculo
Skeleton - Esqueleto / **Bone** - Hueso
Spine - Columna vertebral / **Ribs** - Costillas / **Skull** - Cráneo
Skin - Piel
Vein - Vena

In the human body, the chest is located below the shoulders
En el cuerpo humano, el pecho está debajo de los hombros.
He has a problem with his stomach.
Él tiene un problema con su estómago.
I need to strengthen my arms and legs.
Necesito fortalecer mis brazos y piernas.
I accidentally hit his wrist with my elbow.
Accidentalmente golpeé su muñeca con mi codo.
I have pain in every part of my body especially in my hand, ankle, and back.
Me duelen todas las partes de mi cuerpo, especialmente mi mano, tobillo y espalda.
I want to cut my fingernails and my toenails
Tengo que cortarme las uñas de las manos y los pies.
I need a new bandage for my thumb.
Necesito un vendaje nuevo para mi pulgar.
I have muscle and joint pains.
Tengo dolor de los músculos y las articulaciones.
You should change the cast on your foot at least once a month.
Debes cambiar el yeso (cast) en tu pie por los menos una vez al mes.
The spine is an important part of the skeleton.
La columna vertebral es la parte importante del esqueleto.
I have beautiful skin.
Tengo una piel bonita.
The brain, heart, kidney, lungs, and liver are internal organs.
El cerebro, el corazón, los riñones, los pulmones y el hígado son órganos internos.

HEALTH AND MEDICAL - SALUD Y MÉDICO

Disease - Enfermedad
Bacteria - Bacteria
Sick - Enfermo
Clinic - Clínica
Headache - Dolor de cabeza
Earache - Dolor de oídos
Pharmacy - Farmacia / **Prescription** - Prescripción
Symptoms - Síntomas
Nausea - Náusea / **Stomachache** - Dolor de estómago
Allergy - Alergia
Antibiotic - Antibiótico / **Penicillin** - Penicilina
Sore throat - Dolor de garganta / **Fever** - Fiebre / **Flu** - Gripe
To cough - Toser / **A cough** - Tos
Infection - Infección
Injury - Lesión / **Scar** – Cicatriz / **Ache, pain** - Dolor
Intensive care - Cuidados intensivos
Bandage - Vendaje

Are you in good health?
¿Estás en buena salud?
These bacteria caused this disease.
Estas bacterias causaron esta enfermedad.
He is very sick.
Él está muy enfermo.
I have a bad headache today so I must go to the pharmacy to refill my prescription.
Hoy me duele mucho la cabeza, así que debo ir a la farmacia para rellenar mi receta.
The main symptoms of food poisoning are nausea and stomach ache.
Los síntomas principales de intoxicación alimentaria son náuseas y dolor de estómago.
I have an allergy to penicillin, so I need another antibiotic.
Soy alérgico a la penicilina, por eso necesito otro antibiótico.
What do I need to treat an earache?
¿Qué necesito para tratar un dolor de oído?
I need to go to the clinic for my fever and sore throat.
Necesito ir a la clínica por la fiebre y dolor de garganta.
The bandage won't help your infection.
El vendaje no ayudará tu infección.
I have a serious injury so I must go to intensive care.
Tengo una lesión muy grave, así que debo ir al centro de cuidados intensivos.
I have muscle and joint pains today.
Hoy tengo dolor de los músculos y las articulaciones.

Hospital - Hospital
Doctor - Doctor
Nurse - Enfermera
Family Doctor - Médico de familia / **Pediatrician** - Pediatra
Medicine / medication - Medicina / medicación, **Pills** - Pastillas / píldoras
Heartburn - Acidez
Paramedic – Paramédico / **Emergency room** - Sala de emergencias
Health insurance - Seguro de salud / seguro médico
Patient - Paciente
Surgery - Cirugía / **Surgeon** - Cirujano
Anesthesia - Anestesia
Local anesthesia - Anestesia local / **General anesthesia** - Anestesia general
Wheelchair - Silla de ruedas / **A walker** - Un caminante / **A cane** - Un bastón
Stretcher - Camilla
Dialysis - Diálisis / **Insulin** - Insulina
Temperature - Temperatura / **Thermometer** - Termómetro
A shot - Inyección / **Needle** - Aguja / **Syringe** - Jeringuilla

Where is the closest hospital?
¿Dónde está el hospital más cercano?
I am seeing the nurse now before the doctor.
Estoy viendo a la enfermera ahora antes del doctor.
The paramedics can take her to the emergency room but she doesn't have health insurance.
Los paramédicos pueden llevarla a la sala de emergencias, pero no tiene seguro médico.
The doctor told the patient to go home.
El doctor dijo al paciente que se vaya a su casa.
He needs knee surgery.
Necesita cirugía de la rodilla (knee).
The surgeon requires general anesthesia in order to operate.
El cirujano requiere anestesia general para poder operar.
Does the patient need a wheelchair or a stretcher?
¿El paciente necesita una silla de ruedas o una camilla?
I have to take medicine every day.
Tengo que tomar medicamentos todos los días.
Do you have any pills for heartburn?
¿Tienes alguna píldora para la acidez estomacal?
Where is the closest dialysis center?
¿Dónde está el centro de diálisis más cercano?
Where can I buy insulin for my diabetes?
¿Dónde puedo comprar insulina para mi diabetes?
I need a thermometer to take my temperature.
Necesito un termómetro para tomarme la temperatura.

Health and Medical

Stroke - Derrame cerebral
Blood - Sangre / **Blood pressure** - Presión sanguínea
Heart attack - Ataque de corazón
Cancer - Cáncer / **Chemotherapy** - Quimioterapia
To help - Ayudar
Germs - Gérmenes / **Virus** - Virus
Vaccine - Vacuna / **A cure** - Una cura / **To cure** - Curar
Cholesterol - Colesterol / **Nutrition** - Nutrición / **Diet** - Dieta
Blind - Ciego / **Deaf** - Sordo / **Mute** - Mudo
Nursing home - Asilo de ancianos
Disability - Invalidez / **Handicap** - Desventaja / **Paralysis** - Parálisis
Depression - Depresión / **Anxiety** - Ansiedad
Dentist - Dentista
X-ray - Radiografía
Cavity - Cavidad
Tooth paste - Pasta dental / **Tooth brush** - Cepillo de dientes
Fat (person) - Gordo, **(f)** gorda / **The fat** - La grasa
Skinny - Flaco, **(f)** flaca / **Thin** - Delgado, **(f)** delgada
Young - Joven / **Elderly** - Anciano

A stroke is caused by a lack of blood flow to the brain.
Un derrame cerebral es causado por la falta de flujo sanguíneo en el cerebro.
These are the symptoms of a heart attack.
Estos son los síntomas de un ataque de corazón.
Chemotherapy is used to treat cancer.
La quimioterapia se usa para tratar el cáncer.
Proper nutrition is very important and you must avoid foods that are high in cholesterol.
Una adecuada nutrición es muy importante y debe evitar los alimentos con alto contenido de colesterol.
I need to go on a diet.
Necesito ponerme en dieta.
There is no cure for this virus, only a vaccine.
No hay cura para este virus, solamente una vacuna.
The nursing home is open 365 days a year.
El hogar de ancianos está abierto los 365 días del año.
I don't like suffering from depression and anxiety.
No me place sufrir de depresión y ansiedad.
Soap and water kill germs.
El jabón y el agua matan los gérmenes.
The dentist took X-rays of my teeth to check for cavities.
En el dentista toma radiografías para revisar las cavidades en los dientes.
My toothpaste has the same colors as my toothbrush.
Mi pasta dentífrica tiene los mismos colores que mi cepillo.

EMERGENCY & DISASTERS - EMERGENCIA Y DESASTRES

Help - Ayuda
Fire - Incendio
Ambulance - Ambulancia
First aid - Auxilios primeros / **CPR** - RCP
Emergency number - Número de emergencia
Accident - Accidente
A car accident - Un accidente automovilístico
Death - Muerte / **Deadly** - Mortal / **Fatal** - Fatal
Lightly wounded - Levemente herido
Moderately wounded - Moderadamente herido
Seriously wounded - Gravemente herido
Fire truck - Camión de bomberos / **Siren** – Sirena / **Fire extinguisher** - Extintor
Police - Policía / **Police station** - Estación de policía
Robbery – Robo / **Thief** - Ladrón

There is a fire. I need to call for help.
Hay un incendio. Necesito ayuda.
I need to call an ambulance.
Tengo que llamar a una ambulancia.
That accident was bad.
Ese accidente fue malo.
The thief wants to steal my money.
El ladrón quiere robar mi dinero.
The car crash was fatal. In addition, to the two deaths, four others suffered serious injuries, one was moderately wounded, and two were lightly wounded.
El accidente automovilístico fue fatal. Además de las dos muertes, otros cuatros sufrieron graves heridas, una fue moderadamente y dos resultaron levemente heridas.
To know how to perform CPR is a very important first-aid knowledge.
Saber cómo realizar la RCP es un conocimiento muy importante de auxilios primeros. **What's the emergency number in this country?**
¿Cuál es el número de emergencia en este país?
The police are on their way.
La policía está en camino.
I must call the police station to report a robbery.
Tengo que llamar la policía para denunciar un robo.
The siren of the fire truck is very loud.
La sirena del camión de bomberos es muy ruidosa.
Where is the fire extinguisher?
¿Dónde está el extintor de incendios?

Fire hydrant - La boca de incendio
Fireman - Bombero
Emergency situation - Situación de emergencia
Explosion - Explosión
Rescue - Rescate
Natural disaster - Desastre natural
Destruction - Destrucción / **Damage -** Daño
Hurricane - Huracán
Tornado - Tornado
Hurricane shelter - Refugio contra huracanes
Flood - Inundio
Storm - Tormenta
Snowstorm - Nevada / tormenta de nieve
Hail - Granizo
Refuge - Refugio
Caused - Causó
Safety - La seguridad
Drought - Sequía
Famine - Hambruna
Poverty - Pobreza
Epidemic - Epidemia / **Pandemic -** Pandemia

It's prohibited to park by the fire hydrant in case of a fire.
Es prohibido estacionarse al lado de una boca de incendio, en caso de un incendio.
When there is a fire, the first to arrive on scene are the firemen.
En un incendio los primeros a llegar son los bomberos.
There is a fire. I need to call for help.
Hay un incendio. Necesito ayuda.
In an emergency situation everyone needs to be rescued.
En una situación de emergencia cada uno necesita rescatarse.
The gas explosion led to a natural disaster.
La explosión del gas causo a un desastre natural.
We used the hurricane shelter as refuge.
Utilizamos el refugio debido al huracán.
The hurricane caused a lot of destruction and damage in its path.
El huracán causó mucha destrucción y daño a su paso.
The tornado destroyed the town.
El tornado destruyó la ciudad.
The drought led to famine and a lot of poverty.
La sequía provocó hambre y mucha pobreza.
There were three days of floods following the storm.
Hubo tres días de inundaciones después de la tormenta.
This is a snowstorm and not a hail storm.
Esta es una tormenta de nieve y no de granizo.

Emergency & Disaster

Dangerous - Peligroso
Danger - Peligro
Warning - Advertencia
Earthquake - Terremoto
Disaster - Desastre
Disaster area - Área de desastre
Evacuation - Evacuación
Mandatory - Obligatorio
Safe place - Lugar seguro
Blackout - Apagón
Rainstorm - Tormenta de lluvia
Lightning - Rayo / relámpago
Thunder - Trueno
Avalanche - Avalancha
Heatwave - Ola de calor
Rip current - Corriente de resaca
Tsunami - Tsunami
Whirlpool - Remolino

We need to stay in a safe place during the earthquake.
Necesitamos permanecer en un lugar seguro durante el terremoto.
Heatwaves are usually in the summer.
Las olas de calor suelen ser en el verano.
This is a disaster area, therefore there is a mandatory evacuation order.
En la área del desastre, la evacuación es mandatoria.
There was a blackout for three hours due to the rainstorm.
Tuvimos un apagón durante tres horas debido a la tormenta.
Be careful during the snowstorm since there might be the risk of an avalanche.
Ten cuidado durante la nevada porque puede existir el riesgo de avalancha.
There is a tsunami warning today.
Hoy hay una alerta de tsunami.
You can't swim against a rip current.
No puedes nadar contra una corriente de resaca.
There is a deadly whirlpool in the ocean.
Hay un remolino mortal en el océano.

HOME - CASA / HOGAR

House - Casa
Living room - Sala
Couch - Diván
Sofa - Sofá
Door - Puerta
Closet - Armario
Stairway - Escalera
Rug - Alfombra
Curtain - Cortina
Window - Ventana
Floor - Suelo
Floor (as in level) - Nivel / piso
Fireplace / Chimney - Chimenea
Candle - Vela
Laundry detergent - Detergente
Laundry - Lavandería

He has a fireplace at his home.
El tiene una chimenea en su casa.
The living room is missing a couch and a sofa.
Al salón le faltan un diván y un sofá.
I must buy a new door for my closet.
Debo comprar una nueva puerta para mi armario.
The spiral staircase is beautiful.
La escalera de caracol es hermosa.
There aren't any curtains on the windows.
No hay cortinas en las ventanas.
I have a marble floor on the first floor and a wooden floor on the second floor.
Tengo un suelo de mármol en el primer piso y uno de madera en el segundo.
I can only light this candle now.
Ahora puedo solo encender esta vela.
I can clean the floors today and then I want to arrange the closet.
Hoy puedo limpiar los pisos y luego quiero arreglar el armario.
I need to wash the rug today with laundry detergent and then hang it to dry.
Necesito lavar la alfombra hoy con detergente para ropa y luego colgarla para que se seque.

Silverware - El cubierto
Knife - El cuchillo
Fork - El tenedor
Spoon - La cuchara
Teaspoon - La cucharita
Kitchen - Cocina
A cup - Una taza
Plate - Plato
Bowl - Tazón
Napkin - Servilleta
Table - La mesa
Placemat - Mantel individual
Table cloth - Un mantel
Glass (material) - Vidrio
A glass (cup) - Un vaso
Oven - Horno
Stove - Estufa
Pot (cooking) – Olla / **Pan** - Sartén
Shelve - Estantería
Cabinet - Gabinete
Pantry - Despensa
Drawer - Cajón

The knives, spoons, teaspoons, and forks are inside the drawer in the kitchen.
Los cuchillos, cucharas, cucharaditas y tenedores están dentro del cajón de la cocina.
There aren't enough cups, plates, and silverware on the table for everyone.
No hay suficientes tazas, platos y cubiertos en la mesa para todos.
The napkins are underneath the bowls.
Las servilletas están debajo de los tazones.
I need to set the placemats on top of the table cloth.
Necesito colocar los manteles individuales sobre el mantel.
There is canned food in the pantry.
Hay comida enlatada (canned) en la despensa.
Where are the toothpicks?
¿Dónde están los palillos de dientes?
Can I use wine glasses on the shelf for the champagne?
¿Puedo utilizar copas de vino en el estante para el champán?
The pizza is in the oven.
La pizza esta en el horno.
The pots and pans are in the cabinet.
Las ollas y las sartenes están en el gabinete.
The stove is broken.
La estufa está rota (broken).

Basic Grammatical Requirements of the Spanish Language

Bedroom - Dormitorio
Bed - Cama
Blanket - Manta
Bed sheet - Sábana
Mattress - Colchón
Pillow - Almohada
Mirror - Espejo
Chair - Silla
Dinning room - Comedor
Hallway - Pasillo
Towel - Toalla
Bathtub - Bañera
Shower - Ducha
Sink - Lavabo
Soap - Jabón
Bathroom - Baño
Bag - Bolso / **Box** - Caja
Keys - Llaves

The master bedroom is at the end of the hallway, and the dining room is downstairs.
El dormitorio principal está al final del pasillo y el comedor está abajo.
The mirror looks good in the bedroom.
El espejo se ve bien en el dormitorio.
I have to buy a new bed and a new mattress.
Tengo que comprar una cama nueva y un colchón nuevo.
Where are the blankets and bed sheets?
¿Dónde están las mantas y las sábanas?
My pillows are on the chair.
Mis almohadas están encima (on top) de la silla.
These towels are for drying your hand.
Estas toallas son para secarse sus manos.
The bathtub, shower, and the sink are new.
La bañera, la ducha y el lavabo son nuevos.
I need soap to wash my hands
Necesito jabón para lavar mis manos
The guest bathroom is in the corner of the hallway.
El baño de huéspedes (guests) está en la esquina (corner) del pasillo.
How many boxes does he have?
¿Cuántas cajas tiene él?
I want to put my items in the plastic bag.
Quiero poner mis artículos en la bolsa de plástico.
I need to bring my keys with me.
Necesito traer mis llaves conmigo.

Room - Habitación
Balcony - Balcón
Roof - Techo
Ceiling - Techo
Wall - Pared
Carpet - Tapete
Attic - Ático
Basement - Sótano
Trash - Basura
Garbage can - Contenido de basura
Driveway - Entrada de autos
Garden / backyard - Jardín
Doormat - Felpudo
Jar - Frasco / tarro

I can install new windows for my balcony.
Puedo instalar nuevas ventanas para mi balcón.
I must install a new roof.
Voy a instalar un nuevo techo.
The color of my ceiling is white.
El color de mi techo es blanco.
I must paint the walls.
Tengo que pintar las paredes.
The attic is an extra room in the house.
El ático es una habitación adicional de la casa.
The kids are playing either in the basement or the backyard.
Los niños juegan en el sótano o en el jardín.
All the glass jars are outside on the doormat.
Todos los frascos de vidrio están afuera sobre el felpudo.
The garbage can is blocking the driveway.
El bote de basura está bloqueando el camino de entrada

Conclusion

You have now learned a wide range of sentences in relation to a variety of topics such as the home and garden. You can discuss the roof and ceiling of a house, plus natural disasters like hurricanes and thunderstorms.

The combination of sentences can also work well when caught in a natural disaster and having to deal with emergency issues. When the electricity gets cut you can tell your family or friends, "I can only light this candle now." As you're running out
of the house, remind yourself of the essentials by saying, "I need to bring my keys with me."

If you need to go to a hospital, you have now been provided with sentences and the vocabulary for talking to doctors and nurses and dealing with surgery and health issues. Most importantly, you can ask, "What is the emergency number in this country?" When you get to the hospital, tell the health services, "The hurricane caused a lot of destruction and damage in its path," and "We used the hurricane shelter for refuge."

The three hundred and fifty words that you learned in part 1 should have been a big help to you with these new themes. When learning the Spanish language, you are now more able to engage with people in Spanish, which should make
your travels flow a lot easier.

Part 3 will introduce you to additional topics that will be invaluable to your journeys. You will learn vocabulary in relation to politics, the military, and the family. The three books in this series all together provide a flawless system
of learning the Spanish language. When you visit Spain or Latin America you will now have the capacity for greater conversational learning.

When you proceed to Part 3 you will be able to expand your vocabulary and conversational skills even further. Your range of topics will expand to the office environment, business negotiations and even school.

Please, feel free to post a review in order to share your experience or suggest feedback as to how this method can be improved.

Conversational Spanish Quick and Easy
The Most Innovative Technique to Learn the Spanish Language

Part III

YATIR NITZANY

Translated by:
Semadar Mercedes Friedman

Interior Design:
Menachem Otto

Introduction to the Program

You have now reached Part 3 of Conversational Spanish Quick and Easy. In Part 1 you learned the 350 words that could be used in an infinite number of combinations. In Part 2 you moved on to putting these words into sentences. You learned how to ask for help when your house was hit by a hurricane and how to find the emergency services. For example, if you need to go to a hospital, you have now been provided with sentences and the vocabulary for talking to doctors and nurses and dealing with surgery and health issues. When you get to the hospital, you can tell the health services, "The hurricane caused a lot of destruction and damage in its path," and "We used the hurricane shelter for refuge."

In this third book in the series, you will find the culmination of this foreign language course that is based on a system using key phrases used in day-to-day life. You can now move on to further topics such as things you would say in an office. This theme is ideal if you've just moved to Spanish for a new job. You may be about to sit at your desk to do an important task assigned to you by your boss but you have forgotten the details you were given. Turn to your colleagues and say, "I have to write an important email but I forgot my password." Then, if the reply is "Our secretary isn't here today. Only the receptionist is here but she is in the bathroom," you'll know what is being said and you can wait for help. By the end of the first few weeks, you'll have at your disposal terminology that can help reflect your experiences. "I want to retire already," you may find yourself saying at coffee break on a Monday morning after having had to go to your bank manager and say, "I need a small loan in order to pay my mortgage this month."

I came up with the idea of this unique system of learning foreign languages as I was struggling with my own attempt to learn Spanish. When playing around with word combinations I discovered 350 words that when used together could make up an infinite number of sentences. From this beginning, I was able to start speaking in a new language. I then practiced and found that I could use the same technique with other languages, such as French, Portuguese, Italian and Arabic. It was a revelation.

This method is by far the easiest and quickest way to master other languages and begin practicing conversational language skills.

The range of topics and the core vocabulary are the main components of this flawless learning method. In Part 3 you have a chance to learn how to relate to people in many more ways. Sports, for example, are very important for keeping

Introduction to the Program

healthy and in good spirits. The social component of these types of activities should not be underestimated at all. You will, therefore, have much help when you meet some new people, perhaps in a bar, and want to say to them, "I like to watch basketball games," and "Today are the finals of the Olympic Games. Let's see who wins the World Cup."

For sports, the office, and for school, some parts of conversation are essential. What happens when you need to get to work but don't have any clean clothes to wear because of malfunctions with the machinery. What you need is to be able to pick up the phone and ask a professional or a friend, "My washing machine and dryer are broken so maybe I can wash my laundry at the public laundromat." When you finally head out after work for some drinks and meet a nice new man, you can say, "You can leave me a voicemail or send me a text message."

Hopefully, these examples help show you how reading all three parts of this series in combination will prepare you for all you need in order to boost your conversational learning skills and engage with others in your newly learned language. The first two books have been an important start. This third book adds additional vocabulary and will provide the comprehensive knowledge required.

OFFICE - OFICINA

Boss - (male) Jefe **/ (female)** jefa
Employee - Empleado **/ (female)** empleada
Staff - Personal
Meeting - Reunión / encuentro
Conference room - Sala de conferencias
Secretary – Secretario, **(f)** secretaria **/ Receptionist -** Recepcionista
Schedule - Calendario **/ Calendar -** Calendario
Supplies - Suministros
Pen - Bolígrafo / pluma **/ Ink -** Tinta
Pencil - Lápiz **/ Eraser -** Borrador
Desk - Escritorio **/ Cubicle –** Cubículo **/ Chair -** Silla
Office furniture - Muebles de oficina
Business card - Tarjeta de visita
Lunch break - Pausa para almorzar
Days off - Días de descanso
Briefcase - Maletín
Bathroom - Cuarto de baño

My boss asked me to hand in the paperwork.
Mi jefe me pidió que entrege el papeleo.
Our secretary isn't here today. The receptionist is here but she is in the bathroom.
Nuestra secretaria no está aquí hoy. La recepcionista está aquí pero ella está en el baño.
The employee meeting can take place in the conference room.
La reunión de empleados puede tener lugar en la sala de conferencias.
My business cards are inside my briefcase.
Mis tarjetas de visita están dentro de mi maletín.
The office staff must check their work schedule daily.
El personal de la oficina debe verificar su horario de trabajo diariamente.
I am going to buy office furniture.
Voy a comprar muebles de oficina.
There isn't any ink in this pen.
No hay tinta en este bolígrafo.
This pencil is missing an eraser.
A este lápiz le falta un borrador.
Our days off are written on the calendar.
Nuestros días libres están escritos en el calendario.
I need to buy extra office supplies.
Necesito comprar suministros adicionales de oficina.
I am busy until my lunch break.
Estoy ocupado hasta mi pausa de almuerzo.

Office

Laptop - Ordenador portátil / computadora portátil
Computer - Computadora / ordenador
Keyboard - Teclado
Mouse - Ratóncito
Email - Correo electrónico / e-mail
Password - Contraseña
Attachment - Adjunto archivo
Printer - Impresora
Colored printer - Impresora a color
To download - Descargar
To upload - Cargar
Internet - Internet
Account - Cuenta
A copy - Copia / **To copy -** Copiar
Cut and paste - Cortar y pegar
Fax - Fax
Scanner - Escáner / **To scan -** Escanear
Telephone - Teléfono
Charger - Cargador / **To charge -** Cargar

I have to write an important email but I forgot my password for my account.
Tengo que escribir un correo electrónico importante pero olvidé la contraseña de mi cuenta.
I need to purchase a computer, a keyboard, a printer, and a desk.
Necesito comprar una computadora, un teclado, una impresora y un escritorio.
Where is the mouse on my laptop?
¿Dónde está el ratóncito en mi computadora portátil?
The internet is slow today therefore it's difficult to upload or download.
Hoy el Internet esta lento, por lo tanto, es difícil de cargar o descargar.
Do you have a colored printer?
¿Tienes una impresora a color?
I needed to fax the contract but instead, I decided to send it as an attachment in the email.
Necesitaba enviar el contrato por fax, pero decidí enviarlo como un archivo adjunto al correo electrónico.
One day, the fax machine will be completely obsolete.
Un día, la máquina de fax quedará completamente obsoleta.
Where is my phone charger?
¿Dónde está el cargador de mi teléfono?
The scanner is broken.
El escáner está roto.
The telephone is behind the chair.
El teléfono está detrás de la silla.

Shredder - Trituradora / destructora de documentos
Copy machine - Maquina de copiar
Filing cabinet - Archivador
Paper - Papel / **Page -** Página
Paperwork - Papeleo
Portfolio - Portafolio
Files - Archivos
Document - Documento
Contract - Contrato
Records - Registros
Archives - Archivos
Deadline - Fecha límite
Binder - Aglutinante
Paper clip - Sujeta papeles
Stapler - Engrapadora / **Staples -** Grapas
Stamp - Sello
Mail - Correo
Letter - Carta
Envelope - Sobre
Data - Dato / informacion
Analysis - Análisis
Highlighter - Resaltador / **Marker -** Marcador / **To highlight -** Resaltar
Ruler - Regla

The supervisor at our company is responsible for data analysis.
El supervisor de nuestra empresa es responsable del análisis de datos.
The copy machine is next to the telephone.
La copiadora está al lado del teléfono.
The ruler is next to the shredder.
La regla está al lado de la trituradora.
I can't find my stapler, paper clips, nor my highlighter in my cubicle.
No puedo encontrar mi grapadora, clips de papel, ni mi marcador en mi cubículo.
The filing cabinet is full of documents.
El archivador está lleno de documentos.
The garbage can is full of papers.
El basurero está lleno de papeles.
Give me the file because today is the deadline.
Dame el archivo porque hoy es la fecha límite.
Where do I put the binder?
¿Dónde pongo la carpeta?
I need a stamp and an envelope.
Necesito un sello y un sobre.
There is a letter in the mail.
Hay una carta en el correo.

SCHOOL - ESCUELA

Student - Estudiante
Teacher - Profesor / **(f)** profesora, maestro / **(f)** maestra
Substitute teacher - Profesor sustituto / **(f)** Profesor sustituta
A class - Una clase
A classroom - Un aula
Education - Educación
Private school - Escuela privada
Public school - Escuela publica
Elementary school - Escuela primaria
Middle school - Escuela intermedia
High school - Escuela secundaria
University - Universidad / **College** - Colegio
Grade (level) - Grado / **Grade** (grade on a test) - Calificacione / nota
Pass - Pasó / **Fail** - Falló
Absent - Ausente / **Present** - Presente

The classroom is empty.
El aula está vacía.
I want to bring my laptop to class today.
Quiero llevar mi computadora portátil a la clase hoy.
Our math teacher is absent and therefore a substitute teacher replaced him.
Nuestro professor de matemáticas está ausente, y por lo tanto, un profesor sustituto lo reemplazó.
All the students are present.
Todos los estudiantes están presentes.
Make sure to pass your classes because you can't fail this semester.
Asegúrate de aprobar tus clases porque no puedes reprobar este semestre.
The education level at a private school is much more intense.
El nivel educativo en una escuela privada es mucho más intenso.
I went to a public elementary and middle school.
Fui a la escuela primaria y escuela secundaria pública.
I have good memories of high school.
Tengo buenos recuerdos de la escuela secundaria.
You must get good grades on your report card.
Debe obtener buenas calificaciones en su boleta de calificaciones.
My son is 15 years old and he is in the ninth grade.
Mi hijo tiene 15 años y está en noveno grado.
College textbooks are expensive.
Los libros de texto universitarios son caros.
I want to study at an out-of-state university.
Quiero estudiar en una universidad fuera del estado.

Subject - Tema
Science - Ciencias / **Chemistry** - Química / **Physics** - Física
Geography - Geografía
History - Historia
Math - Matemáticas
Addition - Adición
Subtraction - Sustracción
Division - División
Multiplication - Multiplicación
Language - Idioma / **English** - Inglés / **Foreign language** - Idiomas extranjeros
Physical education - Educación Física
Chalk - Tiza / **Board** - Pizarra
Report card - Boleta de calificaciones
Alphabet - Alfabeto / **Letters** - Letras / **Words** - Palabras
To review - A revisar
Dictionary - Diccionario
Detention - Detención
The principle - El director de la escuela

At school, geography is my favorite subject, English is easy, math is hard, and history is boring.
En la escuela, la geografía es mi materia favorita, el inglés es fácil, las matemáticas son difíciles y la historia es aburrida.
After English class, there is physical education.
Después de la clase de inglés, hay classe de educación física.
Today's math lesson is on addition and subtraction. Next month it will be division and multiplication.
La lección de matemáticas de hoy es sobre suma y resta. El próximo mes será división y multiplicación.
This year for foreign language credits, I want to choose Spanish and French.
Este año para créditos en idiomas extranjeros, quiero elegir español y francés.
I want to buy a dictionary, thesaurus, and a journal for school.
Quiero comprar un diccionario, un diccionario de sinónimos y un periodíco para la escuela.
The teacher needs to write the homework on the board with chalk.
El maestro necesita escribir la tarea en la pizarra con tiza.
Today the students have to review the letters of the alphabet
Hoy los estudiantes tienen que revisar las letras del alfabeto.
The teacher wants to teach roman numerals.
El profesor quiere enseñar los números romanos.
If you can't behave then you must go to the principal's office, and maybe stay after school for detention.
Si no puede comportarse, entonces debe ir a la oficina del director y tal vez quedarse después de la escuela por detención.

School

Test - Examen / **Quiz** - Prueba / cuestionario
Lesson - Lección / **Notes** - Notas
Homework - Tarejas, deberes / **Assignment** - Asignación / **Project** - Proyecto
Pencil - Lápiz / **Pen** - Bolígrafo / **Ink** - Tinta / **Eraser** - Borrador
Backpack - Mochila
Book - Libro / **Folders** - Carpetas / **Notebook** - Cuaderno / **Papers** - Papeles
Calculator — Calculadora
Glue - Pegamento / cola / **Scissors** — Tijeras / **Adhesive tape** - Cinta adhesiva
Lunchbox - Caja de almuerzo / **Lunch** - Almuerzo / **Cafeteria** - Cafetería
Kindergarten - Jardín de infancia / **Pre-school** - Preescolar / **Day care** - Guardería
Triangle - Triángulo / **Square** - Cuadrado / **Circle** - Circulo
Crayons - Lápices de color

Today, we don't have a test but we have a surprise quiz.
Hoy no tenemos un examen, pero tenemos una prueba de sorpresa.
Are a pen, a pencil, and an eraser included with the school supplies?
¿Se incluyen un bolígrafo, un lápiz y un borrador con los útiles escolares?
I think my notepad and calculator are in my backpack.
Creo que mis notas y mi calculadora están en mi mochila.
All my papers are in my folder.
Todos mis papeles están en mi carpeta.
I need glue and scissors for my project.
Necesito pegamento y tijeras para mi proyecto.
I need tape and a stapler to fix my book.
Necesito cinta adhesiva y una grapadora para arreglar mi libro.
You have to concentrate in order to take notes.
Tienes que concentrarte para tomar notas.
The school librarian wants to invite the art and music teacher to the library next week.
El bibliotecario de la escuela quiere invitar al maestro de arte y música a la biblioteca la próxima semana.
For lunch, your children can purchase food at the cafeteria or they can bring food from home.
Para el almuerzo, sus hijos pueden comprar comida en la cafetería o pueden traer comida de casa.
I forgot my lunchbox and crayons at home.
Olvidé mi bolsa de almuerzo y mis crayones en casa.
To draw shapes such as a triangle, square, circle, and rectangle is easy.
Dibujar formas como un triángulo, un cuadrado, un círculo y un rectángulo son fácil.
During the week, my youngest child is at daycare, my middle one is in pre-school, and the oldest is in kindergarten.
Durante la semana, mi hijo menor está en la guardería, mi hijo medino está en la preescolar y el mayor es en la guardería.

PROFESSION - PROFESIÓN

Doctor - Doctor / **(f)** doctora / **Nurse** - Enfermero / **(f)** enfermera
Psychologist - Psicólogo, **(f)** psicóloga / **Psychiatrist** - Psiquiatra, **(f)** psiquiatra
Veterinarian - Veterinario / **(f)** veterinaria
Lawyer - Abogado / abogada / **Judge** - Un juez / **(f)** una jueza
Pilot - Piloto / **Flight attendant** - Azafata
Reporter - Periodista / **Journalist** - Journalista
Electrician - Electricista / **Mechanic** - Mecánico
Investigator - Investigador, **(f)** investigadora / **Detective** - El detective
Translator - Traductor / **(f)** traductora
Producer - Productor / **Director** - Director

What's your profession?
¿Cuál es tu profesión?
I am going to medical school to study medicine because I want to be a doctor.
Voy a la escuela de medicina para estudiar medicina porque quiero ser un médico.
There is a difference between a psychologist and a psychiatrist.
Hay una diferencia entre un psicólogo y un psiquiatra.
Most children want to be an astronaut, a veterinarian, or an athlete.
La mayoría de los niños quieren ser astronautas, veterinarios o atletas.
The judge spoke to the lawyer at the court house.
El juez habló con el abogado en el juzgado.
The police investigator needs to investigate this case.
El investigador policial necesita investigar este caso.
Being a detective could be a fun job.
Ser detective podría ser un trabajo divertido.
The flight attendant and the pilot are on the plane.
La azafata y el piloto están en el avión.
I am a certified electrician.
Soy un electricista certificado.
The mechanic overcharged me.
El mecánico me sobrecargó.
I want to be a journalist.
Quiero ser periodista.
The best translators work at my company.
Los mejores traductores trabajan en mi empresa.
Are you a photographer?
¿Es usted un fotógrafo?
The author wants to hire a ghostwriter to write his book.
El autor quiere contratar a un escritor de fantasmas para que escriba su libro.
I want to find the directors of the company.
Quiero encontrar a los directores de la empresa.

Artist (performer) **-** Artista / ejecutante
Artist (draws paints picture) **-** Artista / dijubador
Author - Autor / **(f)** autora
Painter - Pintor / **(f)** pintora
Dancer - Bailarín / **(f)** bailarina
Writer - Escritor / **(f)** escritora
Photographer - Fotógrafo / **(f)** fotógrafa
A cook - Un cocinero / **(f)** una cocinera
Waiter - Camarero / **(f)** camarera
Bartender - Camarero de bar / **(f)** camarera de bar
Barber - Peluquero / **Barber shop -** La peluqueria, la barbería / **Stylist -** Estilista
Maid - Mucama
Caretaker - Vigilante
Farmer - Campesino / granjero
Gardner - Jardinero
Mailman - Cartero
A guard - Un guardia
A cashier - Un cajero / **(f)** una cajera

The artist drew a sketch.
El artista dibujó un boceto.
The artist produced new artwork for her catalog.
La artista produjo nueva obra de arte para su catálogo.
I want to apply as a cook at the restaurant instead of as a waiter.
Quiero postularme como cocinero en el restaurante en lugar de camarero.
The gardener can only come on weekdays.
El jardinero solo puede venir de lunes a viernes.
I have to go to the barbershop now.
Tengo que ir ala peluquería ahora.
Being a bartender isn't an easy job.
Ser cantinero no es un trabajo fácil.
Why do we need another maid?
¿Por qué necesitamos otra criada?
I need to file a complaint against the mailman.
Necesito presentar una queja contra el cartero.
I am a part-time painter.
Soy pintor a tiempo parcial.
She was a dancer at the play.
Ella era una bailarina en la obra de teatro.
You need to contact the insurance company if you want to find another caretaker.
Debe comunicarse con la compañía de seguros si desea encontrar otro cuidador.
The farmer can sell us ripened tomatoes today.
El campesino puede vendernos tomates maduros hoy.

BUSINESS - NEGOCIO

A business - La empresa, negocio / **Company** - Empresa / **Factory** - Fábrica
A professional - Un profesional
Position - Posición / **Work, job** – Trabajo / **Employee** - Empleado/(f) empleada
Manager - Gerente / **Management** - Administración
Owner - Propietario, (f) propietaria / dueño, (f) dueña
Secretary - Secretario / (f) secretaria
An interview - Una entrevista / **Résumé** - Un currículum
Presentation - Presentación
Specialist - Especialista
To hire - Contratar / **To fire** - Despedir
Pay check - Cheque de pago / **Income** - Ingresos / **Salary** - Salario
Insurance - Seguro / **Benefits** - Beneficios
Trimester - Trimestre / **Budget** - Presupuesto
Net - Neto / **Gross** - Bruto
To retire - Jubilar / **Pension** - Pensión, jubilación

I need a job.
Necesito un trabajo.
She is the secretary of the company.
Ella es la secretaria de la empresa.
The manager needs to hire another employee.
El gerente tiene que contratar otro empleado.
I am lucky because I have an interview for a cashier position today.
Tengo suerte porque hoy tengo una entrevista para un puesto de cajero.
How much is the salary and does it include benefits?
¿Cuánto es el salario e incluye beneficios?
Management has your résumé and they need to show it to the owner of the company.
La administración tiene su currículum y deben mostrárselo al propietario de la empresa.
I am at work at the factory now.
Estoy trabajando en la fábrica ahora.
In business, you should be professional.
En los negocios, debes ser profesional.
Is the presentation ready?
¿Está lista la presentación?
The first trimester is part of the annual budget.
El primer trimestre es parte del presupuesto anual.
I have to see the net and gross profits of the business.
Tengo que ver las ganancias netas y brutas del negocio.
I want to retire already.
Quiero jubilarme ya.

Client – Cliente / **Broker** - Agente/corredor / **Salesperson** - Vendedor
Realtor - Agente inmobiliario / **(f)** agente inmobiliaria
Real estate - Inmobiliario / **Real estate agency** - Agencia inmobiliaria
A purchase - Una compra / **A lease** - Un arrendamiento / **To lease** - Arrendar
To invest - Invertir / **Investment** - Inversión / **Investor** - Inversor
Economy - Economía
Mortgage - Hipoteca / **Interest rate** - Tasa de interés / **A loan** - Un préstamo
Commission - Comisión / **Percent** - Por ciento
A sale - Una venta / **Profit** - Lucro, ganancia, beneficio / **Value** - Valor
Landlord - Dueño, **(f)** dueña / **Tenant** - Inquilino, **(f)** inquilina
The demand - La demanda / **The supply** - El suministro
A contract - Un contrato / **Terms** - Términos
Signature - Firma / **Initials** - Iniciales
Stocks - Acciones / **Stock broker** - Agente de bolsa
Advertisement - Publicidad / **Ads** – Anuncios

I can earn a huge profit from stocks.
Puedo obtener grandes ganancias de las acciones.
The demand in the real estate market depends on the economy.
La demanda en el mercado inmobiliario depende de la economía.
If you want to sell your home, I can recommend a very good realtor.
Si desea vender su casa, le puedo recomendar un muy buen agente inmobiliario.
The investor wants to invest in this shopping center because he says it has good potential.
El inversor quiere invertir en este centro comercial porque dice que tiene un buen potencial.
The value of the property increased by twenty percent.
El valor de la propiedad aumentó en un veinte por ciento.
How much is the commission on the sale?
¿Cuánto es la comisión por la venta?
The client wants to lease instead of purchasing the property.
El cliente quiere arrendar en lugar de comprar la propiedad.
What are the terms of the purchase?
¿Cuáles son los términos de la compra?
I can negotiate a better interest rate.
Puedo negociar una mejor tasa de intereses.
I need a small loan in order to pay my mortgage this month.
Necesito un pequeño préstamo para pagar mi hipoteca este mes.
I need a signature and an initial on the contract.
Necesito una firma y una inicial en el contrato.
My position in the company is marketing and I am responsible for advertising and ads.
Mi posición en la empresa es "marketing" y soy responsable de la publicidad y los anuncios.

Business

Money - Dinero / **Currency -** Moneda
Cash - Efectivo / **Coins -** Monedas
Change (change for a bill) **-** Cambio
Credit - Crédito
Tax - Impuesto
Price - Precio
Invoice - Factura
Inventory - Inventario
Merchandise - Mercancías
A refund - Un reembolso
Product - Producto
Produced - Producido
Retail - Al por menor
Wholesale - Venta al por mayor
Imports - Importaciones / **Exports -** Exportaciones
To ship - Envíar
Shipment - Envío

Don't forget to bring cash with you.
No olvide traer efectivo con usted.
Do you have change for a $100 bill?
¿Tiene usted cambio para una billete de cien dolares?
I don't have a credit card.
No tengo tarjeta de crédito.
The salesperson told me there is no refund.
El vendedor me dijo que no hay reembolso.
This product is produced in Italy.
Este producto se produce en Italia.
I work in the export/import business.
Trabajo en el negocio de exportación y importación.
Let me check my inventory.
Déjame revisar mi inventario.
This product is covered by insurance.
Este producto está cubierto por el seguro.
This invoice contains a mistake.
Esta factura contiene un error.
What is the wholesale and retail value of this shipment?
¿Cuál es el valor mayorista y minorista de este envío?
You don't have enough money to purchase the merchandise.
No tienes suficiente dinero para comprar la mercancía.
How much does the shipping cost and is it in US currency?
¿Cuánto cuesta el envío y es en moneda estadounidense?
There is a tax exemption on this income.
Hay una extensión de impuestos sobre este ingreso.

SPORTS - DEPORTES

Basketball - Baloncesto / **Soccer** - Fútbol / **Baseball** - Béisbol
Game - Juego / **Stadium** - Estadio / **Ball** - Pelota
Player - Un jugador / **(f)** una jugadora
To jump - Saltar / **To throw** - Tirar / **To kick** - Patear / **To catch** - Atrapar
Coach - Entrenador / **(f)** entrenadora / **Referee** - Árbitro
Team - Equipo / grupo / **Teammate** - Compañero de equipo
National team - Selección nacional
Competition – Competencia / **Opponent** - Adversario
Half time - Medio tiempo / **Finals** - Finales
Score - Puntuación / **Scores** - Puntajes
Goal - Objetivo / **The goal** - La meta
To lose - Perder / **A Defeat** - Una derrota / **To win** - Ganar / **A victory** - Una victoria
The looser - El perdedor / **The winner** - El ganador
Fans - Aficionados
Field - Campo
Helmet - Casco / **Basket** - Cesta
A whistle - Un silbato
Penalty - Multa / pena

I like to watch basketball games.
Me gusta ver juegos de baloncesto.
Soccer is my favorite sport.
El fútbol es mi deporte favorito
I have tickets to a football game at the stadium.
Tengo boletos para un juego de fútbol americano en el estadio.
To play basketball, you need to be good at shooting and jumping.
Para jugar baloncesto, debes de ser bueno en disparar y saltar.
The national team has a lot of fans.
El equipo nacional tiene muchos aficionados.
My teammate can't find his baseball helmet.
Mi compañero de equipo no puede encontrar su casco de béisbol.
The coach and the team were on the field during half-time.
El entrenador y el equipo estuvieron en el campo durante el descanso.
The coach needs to bring his team today to meet the new referee.
El entrenador necesita traer a su equipo hoy para conocer al nuevo árbitro.
Our opponents went home after their defeat.
Nuestros oponentes se fueron a casa después de su derrota.
The player received a penalty for kicking the ball in the wrong goal.
El jugador recibió una penalización por patear la pelota en la portería equivocada.
Not every person likes sports.
No a todas las personas les gustan los deportes.

Athlete - El deportista / **(f)** la deportista
Olympics - Juegos Olímpicos / **World cup** - Copa Mundial
Bicycle - Bicicleta / **Cyclist** - Ciclista / **Swimming** - Natación
Wrestling - Lucha / **Boxing** - Boxeo / **Martial arts** - Artes marciales
Championship - Campeonato / **Award** - Premio / **Tournament** - Torneo
Horse racing - Las carreras de caballos / **Racing** - Carreras
Pool (billiards) - Billar / **Pool** (swimming pool) - Piscina
Exercise - Ejercicio / **Fitness** - Aptitud / **Gym** - Gimnasio
Captain - Capitán / **Judge** - Juez, **(f)** jueza
A match - Un combate / **Rules** - Reglas / **Track** - Pista

Today are the finals for the Olympic Games.
Hoy son las finales de los Juegos Olímpicos.
Let's see who wins the World Cup.
Veamos quién gana el Mundial.
I want to compete in the cycling championship.
Quiero competir en el campeonato de ciclismo.
I am an athlete so I must stay in shape.
Soy un atleta, así que debo mantenerme en forma.
After my boxing lesson, I want to go and swim in the pool.
Después de mi clase de boxeo, quiero ir a nadar a la piscina.
He will receive an award because he is the winner of the martial-arts tournament.
Recibirá un premio porque es el ganador del torneo de artes marciales.
The wrestling captain must teach his team the rules of the sport.
El capitán de lucha debe enseñar a su equipo las reglas del deporte.
At the horse-racing competition, the judge couldn't announce the score.
En la competencia de carreras de caballos, el juez no pudo anunciar el puntaje.
There is a bicycle race at the park today.
Hoy hay una carrera de bicicletas en el parque.
This fitness program is expensive.
Este programa de ejercicios es costoso.
It's healthy to go to the gym every day.
Es saludable ir al gimnasio todos los días.
Weightlifting is good exercise.
El levantamiento de pesas es un buen ejercicio.
I want to run on the track today.
Quiero correr en la pista hoy.
I like to win in billiards.
Me encanta ganar en juego de billiard.
Skateboarding is forbidden here.
El skateboard está prohibido aquí.
Skating is much easier than it seems.
Patinar es mucho más fácil de lo que parece.

OUTDOOR ACTIVITIES - ACTIVIDADES AL AIRE LIBRE

Hiking - Excursionismo
Hiking trail - Ruta de senderismo
Pocket knife - Cuchillo de bolsillo
Compass - Brújula
Camping - Campamento
RV - Casa rodante
Campground - Terreno de campamento
Tent - Tienda
Campfire - Hoguera, fogata / **Matches -** Fósforos / **Lighter -** Encendedor
Coal - Carbón
Flame - Fuego
The smoke - El humo
Fishing / to fish - Pescar
Fishing pole - Caña de pesca / **Fishing line -** Línea de pesca / sedal
Hook - Gancho / **A float -** Flotador / **A weight -** Peso / **Bait -** Cebo
Fishing net - Red de pescar
To hunt - Cazar
Rifle - Rifle / escopeta

I enjoy hiking on the trail, with my compass and my pocketknife.
Me encanta ir de excursión por el sendero, con mi brújula y mi navaja.
Don't forget the water bottle in your backpack.
No olvides de poner la botella de agua en tu mochila.
There aren't any tents at the campground.
No hay tiendas de campaña en el campamento.
I want to sleep in an RV instead of a tent.
Quiero dormir en una casa rodante en vez de una tienda.
We can use a lighter to start a campfire.
Podemos usar un encendedor para iniciar una fogata.
We need coal and matches for the camping trip.
Necesitamos carbón y fósforos para el viaje de campamento.
Put out the fire because the flames are very high and there is a lot of smoke.
Apague el fuego porque las llamas son muy altas y hay mucho humo.
There is fog outside and the temperature is below freezing.
Hay neblina afuera y la temperatura esta en bajo cero.
Where is the fishing store? I need to buy hooks, fishing line, bait, and a net.
¿Dónde está la tienda de pesca? Necesito comprar ganchos, sedal, cebo y una red.
You can't bring your fishing pole or your hunting rifle to the campground of the State Park because there is a sign there which says, "No fishing and no hunting."
No puede llevar su caña de pesca o su rifle de caza al campamento del Parque Estatal. Porque hay el letrero dice: "No pescar ni cazar".

Sailing - Navegación
A sail - Una vela
Sailboat - Velero
Rowing - Remo
A paddle - Un remo
Motor - Motor
Canoe - Canoa
Kayak - Kayac
Rock climbing - Escalada de roca
Horseback riding - Cabalgatas
Diver - Buceador / **(f)** buceadora
Scuba diving - Submarinismo
Skydiving - Paracaidismo
Parachute - Paracaídas
Paragliding - Parapente
Hot air balloon - Globo aerostático
Kite - Una cometa
Surfing - Surf
Surf board - Tabla de surf
Ice skating - Patinaje sobre hielo / **Skiing** - Esquiar

With a broken motor, we need a paddle to row the boat.
Con el motor roto, necesitamos una rema para remar el bote.
It's important to know how to use a sail before sailing on a sailboat.
Es importante saber cómo usar una vela antes de navegar en un velero.
In my opinion, a kayak is much more fun than a canoe.
En mi opinión, un kayak es mucho más divertido que una canoa.
Do I need to bring my scuba certification in order to scuba dive at the reef?
¿Necesito traer mi certificación de buceo para bucear en el arrecife?
I have my mask, snorkel, and fins.
Tengo mi máscara, snorkel y aletas.
I don't know which is scarier, sky diving or paragliding.
No sé cuál es más aterrador, paracaidismo o parapente.
There are several outdoor activities here including rock climbing and horseback riding.
Aquí hay varias actividades al aire libre, como escalada en roca y paseos a caballo.
My dream was always to fly in a hot-air balloon.
Mi sueño siempre fue volar en un globo aerostático.
We are going skiing on our next vacation.
Vamos a esquiar en nuestras próxima vacacion.
Where is the surfboard? I want to surf the waves at the beach tomorrow.
¿Dónde está la tabla de surf? Quiero surfear las olas en la playa mañana.
Ice skating is fun.
El patinaje sobre hielo es divertido.

ELECTRICAL DEVICES - APARATOS ELÉCTRICOS

Electric - Eléctrico / **Electricity** - Electricidad / **Electronic** - Electrónica
Appliance - Aparato / electrodoméstico
Oven – Horno / **Stove** - Estufa / **Microwave** - Microondas
Refrigerator - Refrigerador / **Freezer** - Congelador
Coffee maker - Maquina de cafe / **Coffee pot** - Cafetera
Toaster - Tostadora
Dishwasher - Lavavajillas
Laundry machine - Lavadora / **Laundry** - Lavandería
Dryer - Secadora
Fan - Ventilador / **Air condition** - Aire acondicionado
Alarm - Alarma / **Smoke detector** - Detector de humo
Remote control - Control remoto
Battery – Batería

He needs to pay his electric bill if he wants electricity.
Necesita pagar su factura de electricidad si quiere electricidad.
I need to purchase a few things at the electronic store and at the appliance store tomorrow.
Necesito comprar algunas cosas en la tienda electrónica y en la tienda de electrodomésticos mañana.
I can't put plastic utensils in the dishwasher.
No puedo poner utensilios de plástico en el lavavajillas.
I am going to get rid of my microwave and oven because they are not functioning.
Me voy a deshacer de mi microondas y mi horno porque no funcionan.
The refrigerator and freezer aren't cold enough.
El refrigerador y el congelador no están suficientemente fríos.
The coffee maker and toaster are in the kitchen.
La machina de cafe y la tostadora están en la cocina.
My washing machine and dryer do not function therefore I must wash my laundry at the public laundromat.
Mi lavadora y secadora no funcionan, así que tal vez tengo que lavar mi ropa en la lavandería.
Is this fan new?
¿Es este ventilador nuevo?
Unfortunately, the new air conditioner unit hasn't been delivered yet.
Desafortunadamente, la nueva unidad de aire acondicionado aún no se ha entregado.
Is that annoying sound the alarm clock or the fire alarm?
¿Es ese molesto sonido el despertador o la alarma de incendio?
The smoke detector needs new batteries.
El detector de humo necesita baterías.

Lamp - Lámpara
Stereo - Estéreo
A clock / a watch - Un reloj
Vacuum cleaner - Aspiradora
Phone - Teléfono
Text message - Mensaje de texto / **Voicemail** - Mensaje de voz
Camera - Cámara
Flashlight - Linterna / **Light** - Luz
Furnace - Horno / **Heater** - Calentador
Cord - Cordón / **Charger** - Cargador
Outlet - Enchufe
Headsets - Auriculares
Door bell - Timbre de la puerta
Lawn mower - Cortacésped

The clock is hanging on the wall.
El reloj está colgado en la pared.
The cordless stereo is on the table.
El estéreo inalámbrico está sobre la mesa.
I still have a home telephone.
Todavía tengo un teléfono de casa.
I need to buy a lamp and a vacuum cleaner today.
Necesito comprar una lámpara y una aspiradora hoy.
In the past, cameras were more common. Today, everyone can use their phones to take pictures.
En el pasado, las cámaras eran más comunes. Hoy, todos pueden usar sus teléfonos para tomar fotos.
You can leave me a voicemail or send me a text message.
Puedes dejarme un mensaje de voz o enviarme un mensaje de texto.
The lights don't function when there is a blackout therefore I must rely on my flashlight.
Las luces no funcionan cuando hay un apagón, por eso, debo confiar en mi linterna.
I can't hear the doorbell.
No puedo escuchar el timbre.
There is a higher risk of causing a house fire from an electric heater than a furnace.
Existe un mayor riesgo de provocar un incendio en la casa de un calentador eléctrico que un horno.
I need to connect the cord to the outlet.
Necesito conectar el cable al enchufe.
His lawnmower is very noisy.
Su cortadora de césped es muy ruidosa.
Why is my headset on the floor?
¿Por qué mi auricular está en el suelo?

TOOLS - HERRAMIENTAS

Toolbox - Caja de herramientas
Carpenter - Carpintero
Hammer - Martillo
Saw - Sierra / **Axe** - Hacha
A drill - Perforador / **To drill** - Perforar
Nail - Clavo / **A screw** - Un tornillo
Screwdriver - Destornillador / **Pliers** - Alicates / **Wrench** - Llave inglesa
Paint brush - Cepillo de pintura / **To paint** - Pintar / **The paint** - La pintura
Ladder - Escalera
Rope - Cuerda / **String** - Cuerda
A scale - Una escala / **Measuring tape** - Cinta métrica
Machine - Máquina
A lock - Candado / **Locked** - Cerrada / **To lock** - Cerrar
Equipment - Equipo
Metal - Metal / **Steel** - Acero / **Iron** - Hierro
Broom - Escoba / **Dust pan** - El recogedor
Mop - Esponja / trapo / fregona
Bucket - Cubo / **Sponge** - Esponja
Shovel - Pala / **A trowel** - Una paleta

The carpenter needs nails, a hammer, a saw, and a drill.
El carpintero necesita clavos, un martillo, una sierra y un taladro.
The string is very long. Where are the scissors?
La cuerda es muy larga. ¿Dónde están las tijeras?
The screwdriver is in the toolbox.
El destornillador está en la caja de herramientas.
This tool can cut through metal.
Esta herramienta puede cortar metal.
The ladder is next to the tools.
La escalera está al lado de las herramientas.
I must buy a brush to paint the walls.
Debo comprar un pincel para pintar las paredes.
The paint bucket is empty
El cubo de pintura está vacío.
It's better to tie the shovel with a rope in my truck.
Es mejor atar la pala con una soga en mi camioneta.
How can I fix this machine?
¿Cómo puedo arreglar esta máquina?
The broom and dust pan are with the rest of my cleaning equipment.
La escoba y el recogedor están con el resto de mi equipo de limpieza.
Where did you put the mop and the bucket?
¿Dónde pusiste el trapo y el cubo?

CAR - AUTO

Engine - Motor
Ignition - Ignición
Steering wheel - Volante
Automatic - Automático
Manual - Manual
Gear shift - Palanca de cambios / cambio de marchas
Seat - Asiento
Seat belt - Cinturón de seguridad
Airbag - Bolsa de aire
Brakes - Frenos
Hand brake - Freno de mano
Baby seat - Asiento de bebe
Driver seat - Asiento del conductor
Passenger seat - Asiento del pasajero
Front seat - Siento delantero
Back seat - Asiento trasero
Car passenger - Pasajero del coche
Warning light - Luz de alerta
Button - Botón
Horn (of the car) **-** Bocina

When driving, both hands must be on the steering wheel.
Al conducir, ambas manos deben estar en el volante.
I must take my car to my mechanic because there is a problem with the ignition.
Debo llevar mi automóvil a mi mecánico porque hay un problema con el ignición.
What's happened to the engine?
¿Qué le paso al motor?
The seat is missing a seat belt.
Al asiento le falta el cinturón de seguridad.
I prefer a gear shift instead of an automatic car.
Prefiero un cambio de marcha en lugar de un automóvil automático.
The brakes are new in this vehicle
Los frenos son nuevos en este auto.
This vehicle doesn't have a handbreak.
Este vehiculo no tiene un freno de mano.
There is an airbag on both the driver side and the passenger side.
Hay una bolsa de aire tanto en el lado del conductor como en el lado del pasajero.
The baby seat is in the back seat.
El asiento para bebé está en el asiento trasero.
The warning light button is located next to the stirring wheel.
El botón de la luz de advertencia se encuentra al lado del volante.

Windshield - Parabrisas
Windshield wiper - Limpiaparabrisas
Windshield fluid - Líquido parabrisas
Rear view mirror - Espejo retrovisor
Side mirror - Espejo lateral
Door handle - Manija de la puerta
Spare tire - Llanta de repuesto
Trunk - Maletero
Hood (of the vehicle) - Capó del vehículo
Alarm - Alarma
Window - Ventana
Drive license - Licencia de conducir/manejar
License plate - Placa
Gas - Gasolina
Low fuel - Bajo combustible
Flat tire - Llanta desinflado
Crowbar - Palanca
A jack - Un gato

The windshield and all four of my car windows are cracked.
El parabrisas y las cuatro ventanas de mi auto están agrietados.
I want to clean my rear-view mirror and my side mirrors.
Quiero limpiar mi espejo retrovisor y mis espejos laterales.
My car doesn't have an alarm.
Mi auto no tiene alarma.
Does this car have a spare tire in the trunk?
¿Hay una llanta de repuesto en el maletero de este auto?
Please, close the car door.
Por favor, cierra la puerta del auto.
Where is the nearest gas station?
¿Dónde está la gasolinera más cercana?
The windshield wipers are new.
Los limpiaparabrisas son nuevos.
The door handle on the driver's side is broken.
La manija de la puerta del lado del conductor está rota.
Your license plate has expired.
Su placa ha expirado.
I need to renew my driving license today.
Necesito renovar mi licencia de conducir hoy.
Are the car doors locked?
¿Están las puertas del auto cerradas?

NATURE - NATURALEZA

A plant - Una planta
Forest - Bosque
Tree - Árbol / **Wood -** Madera
Trunk - Tronco / **Branch -** Rama / **Leaf -** Hoja / **Root -** Raíz
Flowers - Flores
Petal - Pétalo
Blossom - Florecer
Stem - Tallo / **Seed -** Semilla
Rose - Rosa
Nectar - Néctar / **Pollen -** Polen
Vegetation - Vegetación / **Bush -** Arbusto / **Grass -** Césped
Rain forest - Selva / **Tropical -** Tropical
Palm tree - Palmera / palma
Season - Estaciones del ano
Spring - Primavera / **Summer -** Verano / **Winter -** Invierno / **Autumn -** Otoño

I want to collect a few leaves during the fall.
Quiero recoger algunas hojas durante el otoño.
There aren't any plants in the desert during this season.
No hay plantas en el desierto durante esta temporada.
The trees need rain.
Los árboles necesitan lluvia.
The trunk, the branches, and the roots are all parts of the tree.
El tronco, las ramas y las raíces son todas partes del árbol.
Palm trees can only grow in a tropical climate.
Las palmeras solo pueden crecer en un clima tropical.
My rose bushes are beautiful.
Mis rosales son hermosos.
Where can I plant the seeds?
¿Dónde puedo plantar las semillas?
I must cut the grass and vegetation in my garden.
Debo cortar el césped y la vegetación en mi jardín.
The rain forest is a nature preserve.
La selva tropical es una reserva natural.
I am allergic to pollen.
Soy alérgico/(f) alérgica al polen.
The orchid needs to bloom because I want to see its beautiful petals.
La orquídea tiene que florecer porque quiero ver sus hermosos pétalos.
Is the nectar from the flower sweet?
¿Es el néctar de la flor dulce?
Be careful because the plant stem can break very easily.
Tenga cuidado porque el tallo de la planta puede romperse muy fácilmente.

Lake - Lago
Sea - Mar
Ocean - Oceano
Waterfall - Cascada / cataratas
River - Río / **Canal** - Canal / **Swamp** - Pantano
Mountain - Montaña / **Hill** - Colina / **Cliff** - Acantilado / **Peak** - Pico
Rainbow - Arco iris
Clouds - Nubes
Lightning - Relámpago / **Thunder** - Trueno
Rain - Lluvia / **Snow** - Nieve
Ice - Hielo / **Hail** - Granizo
Fog - Neblina
Wind - Viento / **Air** - Aire
Dawn - Amanecer / **Dew** - Rocío
Sunset - Crepúsculo / **Sunrise** - Alba / salida del sol

There is a rainbow above the waterfall.
Hay un arco iris encima de la cascada.
The ocean is bigger than the sea.
El océano es más grande que el mar.
From the mountain, I can see the river.
Desde la montaña, puedo ver el río.
Today we hope to see snow.
Hoy esperamos ver la nieve.
There aren't any clouds in the sky.
No hay nubes en el cielo.
I see the lightning from my window.
Veo el relámpago desde mi ventana.
I can hear the thunder from outside.
Puedo escuchar el trueno de afuera.
I want to see the sunset from the hill.
Quiero ver el crepúsculo desde la colina.
The lake has a shallow part and a deep part.
El lago tiene una parte poco profunda y una parte profunda.
I don't like the wind.
No me gusta el viento.
The air on the mountain is very clear.
El aire en la montaña esta muy claro.
Every dawn, there is dew on the leaves of my plants.
En cada amanecer, hay rocío en las hojas de mis plantas.
Is this ice or hail?
¿Es esto hielo o granizo?
 I can see the volcano.
Puedo ver el volcan.

Nature

Sky - Cielo
World - Mundo
Earth / ground / soil - Tierra
Sun - Sol / **Moon** - Luna / **Crescent** - Creciente / **Star** - Estrella / **Planet** - Planeta
Fire - Fuego / **Heat** - Calor / **Humidity** - Humedad
Field – Campo / **Agriculture** - Agricultura
Weeds - Malas hierbas
Island - Isla
Cave - Cueva / caverna
Park - Parque / **National park** - Parque nacional
Rock - Roca / **Stone** - Piedra
Sea shore - Orilla del mar / **Seashell** - Concha
Dawn - Amanecer
Ray - Rayo
Dry - Seco / **Wet** - Mojado
Deep - Profundo / **Shallow** - Poco profundo
A stick - Un palo
Dust - Polvo

The moon and the stars are beautiful in the night sky.
La luna y las estrellas son hermosas en el cielo nocturno.
The earth is a planet, and the sun is a star.
La tierra es un planeta y el sol es una estrella.
The heat today is unbearable.
El calor hoy es insoportable.
At the beach there is fresh air.
Hay aire fresco en la playa.
I want to sail to the island to see the sunrise.
Quiero navegar a la isla para ver el amanecer.
Parts of the cave are dry and other parts are wet.
Partes de la cueva están secas y otras partes están mojadas.
We live in a beautiful world.
Vivimos en un mundo hermoso.
There is dust from the fire in the park.
Hay polvo del fuego en el parque.
I want to collect seashells from the seashore.
Quiero recoger conchas de la orilla del mar.
There are too many rocks in the soil so it's impossible to use this area as a field for agricultural purposes.
Hay demasiadas rocas en esta tierra, por eso es imposible utilizar esta área como campo para fines agrícolas.
Why are there so many weeds growing by the swamp?
¿Por qué hay tantas yierbas creciendo junto al pantano?

ANIMALS - ANIMALES

Animals - Animales
Pet - Mascota
Mammal - Mamífero
Cat - Gato / **Dog** - Perro
Parrot - Loro / papagayo
Pigeon - Paloma
Pig - Cerdo
Sheep - Oveja
Cow - Vaca / **Bull** - Toro
Donkey - Burro / **Horse** - Caballo
Camel - Camello
Rodent - Roedor
Mouse - Ratón / **Rat** - Una rata
Rabbit - Conejo / **Hamster** - Hámster
Duck - Pato / **Goose** - Ganso
Turkey - Pavo / **Chicken** - Gallina, **(m)** gallo / **Poultry** - Aves de corral
Squirrel - Ardilla

I have a dog and two cats.
Tengo un perro y dos gatos.
There is a bird on the tree.
Hay un pájaro en el árbol.
I want to go to the zoo to see the animals.
Quiero ir al jardin zoológico para ver a los animales.
My daughter wants a pet horse.
Mi hija quiere un caballo como mascota.
A pig, a sheep, a donkey, and a cow are considered farm animals.
Un cerdo, una oveja, un burro y una vaca se consideran animales de granja.
I want a hamster as a pet.
Quiero un hámster como mascota.
A camel is a desert animal.
Un camello es un animal del desierto.
Can I put ducks, geese, and turkeys inside my chicken coop?
¿Puedo poner patos, gansos y pavos dentro de mi gallinero?
We have rabbits and squirrels in our patio.
Tenemos conejos y ardillas en nuestro patio.
It's cruel to keep a parrot inside a cage.
Es cruel mantener un loro dentro de una jaula.
There are many pigeons in the city.
Hay muchas palomas en la ciudad.
Mice and rats are rodents.
Los ratones y las ratas son roedores.

Lion - León
Hyena - Hiena
Leopard - Leopardo
Panther - Pantera
Cheetah - Guepardo
Elephant - Elefante
Rhinoceros - Rinoceronte
Hippopotamus - Hipopótamo
Bat - Murciélago
Fox - Zorro / **Wolf** - Lobo
Weasel - Comadreja
Bear - Oso
Tiger - Tigre
Deer - Ciervo
Monkey - Mono / (f) mona
Sloth - El mono perezoso
Marsupial - Marsupial

There are a lot of animals in the forest.
Hay muchos animales en el bosque.
The most dangerous animal in Africa is not the lion, it's the hippopotamus.
El animal más peligroso en África no es el león, es el hipopótamo.
A wolf is much bigger than a fox.
Un lobo es mucho más grande que un zorro.
Are there bears in this forest?
¿Hay osos en este bosque?
Bats are the only mammals that can fly.
Los murciélagos son los únicos mamíferos que pueden volar.
It's usually very difficult to see leopards in the wild.
Por lo general, es muy difícil ver leopardos en la naturaleza.
Cheetahs are common in certain regions of Africa.
Los guepardos son comunes en ciertas regiones de África.
Elephants and rhinoceroses are known as very aggressive animals.
Los elefantes y los rinocerontes son conciderados como animales muy agresivos.
I saw a hyena and a panther at the safari yesterday.
Ayer vi una hiena y una pantera en el safari.
The largest member of the cat family is the tiger.
El miembro más grande de la familia de los gatos es el tigre.
Deer hunting is forbidden in the national park.
La caza de ciervos está prohibida en el parque nacional.
There are many monkeys on the branches of the trees.
Hay muchos monos en las ramas de los árboles.
An opossum isn't a rat but it's a marsupial just like the kangaroo.
Una zarigüeya no es una rata, pero es un marsupial al igual que el canguro.

Animals

Bird - Pájaro
Crow - Cuervo
Stork - Cigüeña
Eagle - Águila / **Vulture** - Buitre
Owl - Búho
Peacock - Pavo real
Reptile - Reptil
Turtle - Tortuga
Snake - Serpiente / **Lizard** - Lagartija / **Crocodile** - Cocodrilo
Frog - Rana
Seal - Foca
Whale - Ballena / **Dolphin** - Delfín
Fish - Pescado
Shark - Tiburón
Wing - Ala / **Feather** - Pluma
Tail - Cola
Fur - Piel
Scales - Escamas
Fins - Aletas
Horns - Cuernos
Claws - Garras

Eagles and owls are birds of prey however vultures are scavengers.
Las águilas y los búhos son aves rapaces, sin embargo, los buitres son carroñeros.
Crows are very smart.
Cuervos son muy inteligentes.
I want to see the stork migration in Europe.
Quiero ver la migración de la cigüeña en Europa.
Don't buy a fur coat!
¡No compra un abrigo de piel!
Butterflies and peacocks are colorful.
Las mariposas y los pavos reales son coloridos.
Some snakes are poisonous.
Algunas serpientes son venenosas.
Is that the sound of a cricket or a frog?
¿Es ese el sonido de un grillo o una rana?
Lizards, crocodiles, and turtles belong to the reptile family.
Lagartos, cocodrilos y tortugas pertenecen a la familia de los reptiles.
I want to see the fish in the lake.
Quiero ver los peces en el lago.
There were a lot seals basking on the beach last week.
Muchas focas habían tomando el sol en la playa la semana pasada.
A whale is not a fish.
Una ballena no es un pez.

Insect - Insecto
A cricket - Un grillo
Ant - Hormiga / **Termite** - Termita
A fly - Una mosca
Butterfly - Mariposa
Worm - Gusano
Mosquito - Mosquito / **Flea** - Pulga / **Lice** - Piojo
Beetle - Escarabajo
A roach - Una cucaracha
Bee - Abeja
Spider - Araña / **Scorpion** - Escorpión
Snail - Caracol
Invertebrates - Invertebrados
Shrimps - Camerones / **Clams** - Almejas / **Crab** - Cangrejo
Octopus - Pulpo
Starfish - Estrella de mar
Jellyfish - Medusa

An octopus has eight tentacles.
El pulpo tiene ocho tentáculos.
Jellyfish is a common dish in Asian culture.
En la cultura asiática la medusa es un plato común.
The museum has a large collection of invertebrate fossils.
El museo tiene una gran colección de fósiles de invertebrados.
I want to buy mosquito spray.
Quiero comprar repelente de mosquitos.
I need antiseptic for my bug bites.
Necesito antiséptico para mis mordizcos de insectos.
I hope there aren't any worms, ants, or flies in the bag of sugar.
Espero que no haya gusanos, hormigas o moscas en la bolsa de azúcar.
I have crabs and starfish in my aquarium.
Tengo cangrejos y estrellas de mar en mi acuario.
Certain types of spiders and scorpions can be dangerous.
Ciertos tipos de arañas y escorpiones pueden ser peligrosos.
I need to call the exterminator because there are fleas, roaches, and termites in my house.
Necesito llamar al exterminador porque hay pulgas, cucarachas y termitas en mi casa.
Bees are very important for the environment.
Las abejas son muy importantes para el medio ambiente.
Is there a snail inside the shell?
¿Hay un caracol dentro del caparazón?
Beetles are my favorite insects.
Los escarabajos son mis insectos favoritos.

RELIGION, HOLIDAYS & TRADITION
RELIGIÓN, FIESTAS Y TRADICIONES

God - Dios / **Bible** - Biblia
Old Testament - Viejo Testamento / **New Testament** - Nuevo Testamento
Adam - Adam / **Eve** - Eva / **Garden of Eden** - Jardín del Edén
Heaven - Cielo / **Angels** - Ángeles
To pray - Orar, rezar / **Prayer** - Oración, un rezo
Blessing - Bendición/ **To bless** - Bendecir / **Holy** - Santo / **Faith** - Fe
Moses - Moisés / **Prophet** - Profeta / **Messiah** - Mesías / **Miracle** - Milagro
Ten commandments - Diez Mandamientos
The five books of Moses - Los cinco libros de Moises
Genesis - Génesis / **Exodus** - Éxodo / **Leviticus** - Levítico
Numbers - Números / **Deuteronomy** - Deuteronomio

What is your religion?
¿Cual es tu religion?
Many religions use the chapel.
Muchas religones usan la capilla.
We have faith in miracles.
Tenemos fe en los milagros.
When do I need to say the blessing?
¿Cuándo tengo que decir la bendición?
I must say a prayer for the holiday.
Tengo que decir una oración por las fiestas.
The angels came from heaven.
Los ángeles vinieron del cielo.
Aaron, the brother of Moses, was the first priest.
Aarón, el hermano de Moisés, fue el primer sacerdote.
The story of Noah's Ark and the flood is very interesting.
La historia del Arca de Noé y el diluvio es muy interesante.
Adam and Eve were the first humans and they lived in the Garden of Eden.
Adán y Eva fueron los primeros humanos y vivieron en el Jardín del Edén.
Moses had to climb up on Mount Sinai to receive the Ten Commandments from God.
Moisés tuvo que subir al Monte Sinaí para recibir los Diez Mandamientos de Dios.
The Five Books of the Moses are Genesis, Exodus, Leviticus, Numbers, and Deuteronomy.
Los cinco libros de Moisés son Génesis, Éxodo, Levítico, Números y Deuteronomio.
Moses was considered as the prophet of all prophets.
Moisés fue considerado como el profeta de todos los profetas.
My favorite book of the bible is the Book of Prophets.
Mi libro favorito de la Biblia es el Libro de los Profetas.

Christian Religion - Religión christiano
Church - Iglesia / **Cathedral** - Catedral
Catholic - Católico, **(f)** Católica / **Christian** - Cristiano, **(f)** Cristiana
Christianity - Cristiandad /**Catholicism** - Catolicismo/**Priest** - Sacerdote, padre
Jesus – Jesús / **A cross** - Cruz
Holy - Santo / **Holy water** - Agua bendita
To sin - Pecar / **A sin** - Un pecado
Monastery - Monasterio
Christmas - Navidad/**Christmas tree** - árbol de Navidad/**Christmas eve** - Nochebuena
New Year - Año nuevo / **Merry Christmas** - Feliz Navidad
Easter - Pascuas
Saint - Santo, **(f)** Santa / **Nun** - Monja
Chapel - Capilla
Hell - Infierno / **Devil** - Diablo / **Demons** – Demonios

The church is open today.
La iglesia está abierta hoy.
Christians love to celebrate Christmas.
A los cristianos les encanta celebrar la Navidad.
I need to turn on the lights on my Christmas tree for Christmas Eve.
Necesito encender las luces de mi árbol de Navidad para la víspera de Navidad.
Two more weeks until Easter.
Dos semanas más hasta las Pascuas.
The nuns live in the monastery.
Las monjas viven en el monasterio.
Jesus is the son of God.
Jesús es el hijo de Dios.
I have a gold necklace with a cross.
Tengo un collar de oro con una cruz.
The priest read the Holy Bible in front of the congregation.
El sacerdote leyó la Santa Biblia delante de la congregación.
I went to pray in the cathedral.
Fui a rezar a la catedral.
Merry Christmas and Happy New Year to all my friends and family.
Feliz Navidad y feliz año nuevo a todos mis amigos y familiares.
Peter is a famous saint in Christianity.
Peter es un santo famoso en el cristianismo.
The priest baptized the baby in the blessed holy water.
El sacerdote bautizó al bebé con la agua bendita.
The devil and the demons are from hell.
El diablo y los demonios son del infierno.
Many schools refuse to teach evolution.
Muchas escuelas se niegan a enseñar la evolución.

Religion & Holidays

Jew - Judío / **(f)** Judía
Judaism - Judaísmo
Hanukkah – Januca / **Menorah** - Candelabra de nueve velas
Dreidle - Trompo
Passover - Pascua
Kosher - Casher
Circumcision - Circuncisión
Synagogue - Sinagoga
Goblet - Copa / **Wine** - Vino
Religious - Religioso / **(f)** religiosa
Monotheism - Monoteísmo
Islam - Islam / **Muslim** - Musulmán / **Mohammed** - Mohamed / **Mosque** - Mezquita
Hindu - Hindú / **Buddhist** - Budista / **Temple** – Templo

The Jews worship at the synagogue.
Los judíos rezan en la sinagoga.
The Bible is a holy book which tells the story of the Jewish nations and includes many miracles.
La Biblia es un libro sagrado que cuenta la historia de la nacion judía e incluye muchos milagros.
In Judaism, they pray three times a day. Morning prayer, afternoon prayer, and evening prayer.
En el judaísmo, rezan tres veces al día. Oración de la mañana, oración de la tarde y oración de la noche.
Where is the goblet of wine for Rosh Hashana?
¿Dónde está la copa de vino para Rosh Hashana / el año nuevo de los judios?
The three forefathers are Abraham, Isaac, and Jacob.
Los tres padres antepasados son Abraham, Isaac y Jacob.
I have a menorah and a dreidel for Chanukah.
Tengo una menorá y un trompo para Januca.
Passover is my favorite holiday.
Las pascuas son mi fiesta favorita.
We welcome the Sabbath by lighting candles.
Damos la bienvenida al sábado encendiendo velas.
I want to keep kosher.
Quiero mantenerme casher.
To learn about the Holocaust and the concentration camps is very important.
Aprender sobre el Holocausto y los campos de concentración es muy importante.
Muslims worship at the mosque.
Los musulmanes adoran en la mezquita.
In Islam you must pray five times a day.
En el Islam debes rezar cinco veces al día.

WEDDING AND RELATIONSHIP - BODA Y RELACIÓN

Wedding - Boda
Wedding hall - Salon de bodas
Married - Casado
Civil wedding - Boda civil
Bride - Novia
Groom - Novio
Ceremony - Ceremonia
Reception hall - Pasillo de recepción
Chapel - Capilla
Engagement - Compromiso
Engagement ring - Anillo de compromiso
Wedding ring - Anillo de bodas
Anniversary - Aniversario
Honeymoon - Luna de miel
Fiancé - Prometido / **(f)** prometida
Husband - Marido / esposo
Wife - Mujer/ esposa

They are finally married so now it's time for the honeymoon.
Finalmente están casados, así que ahora es el momento de la luna de miel.
When is the wedding?
¿Cuándo es la boda?
We are having the service in the chapel and the reception in the wedding hall.
Estamos teniendo el servicio en la capilla y la recepción en el salón de bodas.
Our anniversary is on Valentine's Day.
Nuestro aniversario es el día de San Valentín.
This is my engagement ring and this is my wedding ring.
Este es mi anillo de compromiso y este es mi anillo de bodas.
He decided to propose to his girlfriend. She said "yes" and now they are engaged.
Decidió proponerle matrimonio a su novia. Ella dijo "sí" y ahora están comprometidos.
He is my fiancé now. Next year he will be my husband.
Él es mi prometido ahora. El año que viene será mi esposo.
There are three civil weddings at the courthouse today.
Hoy hay tres bodas civiles en el juzgado.
The bride and groom received many presents.
La novia y el novio recibieron muchos regalos.

Valentine day - Día de San Valentín
Love - Amor
In love - Enamorado
To love - Amar
Romantic - Romántico
Darling - Cariño
A date - Una cita
Relationship - Relación
Boyfriend - Novio
Girlfriend - Novia
To hug - Abrazar
A hug - Un abrazo
To kiss - Besar
A kiss - Un beso
Single - Soltero / **(f)** soltera
Divorced - Divorciado / **(f)** divorciada
Widow - Viudo / **(f)** viuda

I am in love with him.
Estoy enamorada de el.
You are very romantic.
Eres muy romantico.
They have a very good relationship.
Tienen una muy buena relación.
I am single because I divorced my wife.
Soy soltero porque me divorcié de mi esposa.
She is my darling and my love.
Ella es mi enamorada y mi amor.
I want to kiss you and hug you in this picture.
Quiero besarte y abrazarte en esta foto.

POLITICS - POLÍTICA

Politics - Política
Flag - Bandera
National anthem - Himno Nacional
Nation - Nación
National - Nacional
International - Internacional
Local - Local
Patriot - Patriota
Symbol - Símbolo
Peace - Paz
Treaty - Trato
State - Estado
County - Condado
Country - País
Century - Siglo
Annexation - Anexión
Plan - Plan
Strategic - Estratégica
Decision - Decisión

This is a political movement which has the support of the majority.
Este es un movimiento político que cuenta con el apoyo de la mayoría.
This flag is the national symbol of the country.
Esta bandera es el símbolo nacional del país.
This is all politics.
Esto es todo política.
There is a difference between state law and local law.
Hay una diferencia entre la ley estatal y la ley local.
He is a patriot of the nation.
Es un patriota de la nación.
Most countries have a national anthem.
La mayoría de los países tienen un himno nacional.
This is a political campaign to demand independence.
Esta es una campaña política para exigir independencia.
The annexation plan was a strategic decision.
El plan de anexión fue una decisión estratégica.

Legal - Legal
Law - Ley
Illegal - Ilegal
International law - Ley internacional
Human rights - Derechos humanos
Punishment - Castigo
Torture - Tortura
Execution - Ejecución
Spy - Espía
Amnesty - Amnistía
Political asylum - Asilo político
Republic - República
Dictator - Dictador
Citizen - Ciudadano
Resident - Residente
Immigrant - Inmigrante
Public - Público
Private - Privado
Racism - Racismo
Government - Gobierno
Revolution - Revolución
Civilian - Civil
Population - Población
Socialism - Socialismo
Communism - Comunismo

In which county is this legal?
¿En qué condado es esto legal?
There were many protests and riots today.
Hubieron muchas protestas y disturbios hoy.
The civilian population wanted a revolution.
La población civil quería una revolución.
The politicians want to ask the president to give the captured spy amnesty.
Los políticos quieren pedirle al presidente que otorgue al espía capturado la amnistía.
Although he was the brutal dictator of the republic, in private he was a nice person.
Aunque era el dictador bruto de la república, en privado era una buena persona.
In some countries torture and execution is a common form of punishment.
En algunos países la tortura y la ejecución son una forma de un castigo común.
This is a violation of human rights and international law.
Esto es una violación de los derechos humanos y el derecho internacional.
Communism and socialism were popular in the 19th century.
El comunismo y el socialismo fuern populares en el siglo dies y nueve.

Politics

President - Presidente
Statement - Declaración
Presidential - Presidencial
Election - Elección
Poll - Encuesta
Campaign - Campaña
Candidate - Candidato
Democracy - Democracia
Movement - Movimiento
Politician - Político
Politics - Política
Campaign - Campaña
To vote - Votar
Majority - Mayoria
Independence - Independencia
Party - Partido
Veto - Veto
Impeachment - El proceso de destitución
Vice president - Vice presidente
Defense Secretary - Secretario de Defensa
Prime minister - Primer ministro
Interior minister - Ministro del Interior
Exterior minister - Ministro del exterior
Convoy - Convoy

They want to appoint him as defense minister.
Quieren nombrarlo como ministro de defensa.
Both parties want to veto the impeachment inquiry.
Ambos partidos quieren vetar la investigación de juicio político.
I want to see the presidential convoy.
Quiero ver el convoy presidencial.
In some countries other than the United States, they have a prime minister, interior minister, and exterior minister.
E n algunos países, fuera de los Estados Unidos, tienen un primer ministro, un ministro del interior y ministro de exteriores.
I want to meet the president and the vice president today.
Quiero reunirme con el presidente y el vicepresidente hoy.
I want to go to the election polls to vote for the new candidate.
Quiero ir a las urnas electorales para votar por el nuevo candidato.
We support democracy and are against fascism and racism.
Apoyamos la democracia y estamos en contra del fascismo y el racismo.

United Nations - Naciones Unidas
Condemnation - Condenación
United States - Estados Unidos
European Union - Unión Europea
Coup - Golpe
Treason - Traición
Fascism - Fascismo
Resistance - Resistencia
Members - Miembros
Captured - Capturado
Ambassador - Embajador
Embassy - Embajada
Consulate - Consulado
Biased - Sesgado
Unilateral - Unilateral
Bilateral - Bilateral
Resolution - Resolución
Rebels - Rebeldes
Sanctions - Sanciones

All the members of the resistance were accused of treason and had to ask for political asylum.
Todos los miembros de la resistencia fueron acusados de traición y tuvieron que pedir asilo político.
The resolution is biased.
La resolución es parcial.
This was an official condemnation.
Esta fue una condena oficial.
The United Nations is located in New York.
Las oficinas de las Naciones Unidas se encuentran en Nueva York.
I am a United States citizen and a resident of the European Union.
Soy ciudadano de los Estados Unidos y residente de la Unión Europea.
The ambassador's residence is located near the embassy.
La residencia del embajador se encuentra cerca de la embajada.
I need the phone number and address of the consulate.
Necesito el número de teléfono y la dirección del consulado.
Are consular services available today?
¿Hay servicios consulares disponibles hoy?
The international peace treaty needs to include both sides.
El tratado de paz internacional debe incluir a ambas partes.
According to the government, the rebels carried out an illegal coup.
Según el gobierno, los rebeldes llevaron a cabo un golpe ilegal.
They must impose sanctions against that country.
Deben imponer sanciones contra ese país.

MILITARY - MILITAR

Army - Ejército / **Armed forces** - Fuerzas armadas
Navy - Marina de guerra
Soldier - Soldado / **Troops** - Tropas
A force - Una fuerza / **Ground forces** - Tropas terrestres
Base - Base / **Headquarter** - Cuartel general / **Intelligence** - Inteligencia
Ranks - Rangos / **Sergeant** - Sargento / **Lieutenant** - Teniente
The general - El general / **Commander** - Comandante / **Captain** - Capitán
Chief of Staff - Jefe de estado mayor
Enlistment - Alistamiento
Reserves - Reservas
War - Guerra
Terrorism - Terrorismo / **Terrorist** - Terrorista / **Insurgency** - Insurrección
Border crossing - Cruce de las fronteras
Refugee - Refugiado
Camp - Campo

I want to enlist in the military.
Quiero enlistrarme en el ejército.
This is a base for military aircrafts only.
Esta es una base solo para aviones militares.
That is the headquarters of the enemy.
Esa es la sede del enemigo.
The Air Force is a branch of the military.
La Fuerza Aérea es una rama de las fuerzas armadas.
They need to enlist reserve forces for the war.
Necesitan reclutar fuerzas de reserva para la guerra.
Welcome to the border crossing.
Bienvenido al cruce de las fronteras.
Military intelligence relies on important sources of information to provide direction and guidance.
La inteligencia militar se basa en importantes fuentes de información para proporcionar dirección y orientación.
The chief of staff was the target of a failed assassination attempt.
El jefe de gabinete fue blanco de un intento fallido de asesinato.
The sniper killed the highest-ranking lieutenant.
El francotirador mató al teniente de más alto rango.
The terrorist group claimed responsibility for the car-bomb attack at the refugee camp.
El grupo terrorista se atribuyó la responsabilidad del ataque con coche bomba en el campo de refugiados.
It's impossible to defeat terrorism because it's an ideology.
Es imposible vencer al terrorismo porque es una ideología.

Air strike - Ataque aéreo
Air force - Fuerza Aerea / **Fighter jet** - Avión de combate
Military aircraft - Aeronave militar
Drone - Zumbido / **Stealth technology** - Tecnología sigilosa
Tank – Tanque / **Submarine** - Submarino
Weapon - Arma
Grenade - Granada / **Mine** - Mía / **Bomb** - Bomba
Sniper - Francotirador / **Gun** - Pistola / **Rifle** - Escopeta, rifle / **Bullet** - Bala
Missile - Misil / **Mortar** - Mortero
Anti tank missile - Misil antitanque / **Anti aircraft missile** - Misil antiaéreo
Shoulder fire missile - Misil de fuego de hombro
Ammunition - Munición / **Artillery** - Artillería
Artillery shell - Proyectil de artillería
Ballistic missile - Misil balístico / **Atomic bomb** - Bomba atómica
Weapon of mass destruction - Arma de destrucción masiva
Chemical weapon - Arma química
Explosion - Explosión
Flare system - Sistema de antorchas
Supply - Suministro / **Storage** - Almacenamiento
Armor - Armadura

The M-16 is a US-made rifle.
El M-16 es un rifle de fabricación estadounidense.
The tank fired artillery shells.
El tanque disparó proyectiles de artillería.
Shoulder-fired missiles are extremely dangerous and are hard to defend against.
Los misiles de hombro son extremadamente peligrosos y son difíciles de defenderse.
The flare system is meant as a defense against anti-aircraft missiles.
El sistema de bengalas pretende ser una defensa contra misiles antiaéreos.
The navy is able to intercept missiles.
La marina puede interceptar misiles.
At the terrorist safe-house, guns, bullets, and grenades were found.
En el refugio de terroristas, se encontraron pistolas, balas y granadas.
The coalition forces struck an enemy arms depot.
Las fuerzas de la coalición atacaron un depósito de armas del enemigo.
An intense missile attack was carried out against the supply forces that resulted in many casualties.
Se llevó a cabo un intenso ataque con misiles contra las fuerzas de suministro que resultó en muchas víctimas.
The terrorist group fired ballistic missiles at the nuclear facility site.
El grupo terrorista disparó misiles balísticos contra el sitio de la instalación nuclear.
Atomic bombs and chemical weapons are weapons of mass destruction.
Las bombas atómicas y las armas químicas son armas de destrucción masiva.

Military

A target - On objetivo / **To target -** Apuntar
An attack - Un ataque / **To attack -** Atacar / **Intense -** Intenso
To shoot - Disparar / **Open fire -** Abran fuego / **Fired -** Despedido
Assassination - Asesinato / **Assassin -** Asesino
Enemy - Enemigo
Reconnaissance - Reconocimiento / **To infiltrate -** Infiltrarse
Invasion - Invasión
Exchange of fire - Intercambio de fuego
A cease fire - Un alto el fuego / **Withdrawal -** Retiro
To defeat – Derrotar / **To surrender -** Rendirse
Victim - Víctima / **Injury -** Lesión / **Wounded -** Herido
Deaths - Muertes / **Killed -** Matado / **To kill -** Matar
Prisoner of war - Prisionero de guerra / **Missing in action -** Perdido en acción
Act of war - Acto de guerra / **War crimes -** Crímenes de guerra
Defense - Defensa
Attempt - Intento

There is an invasion of ground forces.
Hay una invasión de las fuerzas terrestres.
The soldier wanted to open fire and shoot at the invading forces.
El soldado quería abrir fuego y disparó a las fuerzas invasoras.
The bomb attack was considered an act of aggression and an act of war.
El ataque con bomba fue considerado un acto de agresión y un acto de guerra.
The reconnaissance drone managed to infiltrate deep within enemy territory.
El avión no tripulado de reconocimiento logró infiltrarse en las profundidades del territorio enemigo.
The airstrike targeted an ammunition storage site.
El ataque aéreo apuntó a un sitio de almacenamiento de municiones.
The mortar attack and exchange of fire caused injuries and deaths on both sides.
El ataque con mortero y el intercambio de fuego causaron heridas y muerte en ambos lados.
First, we need to clear the mines.
Primero, necesitamos eliminar las minas.
The ceasefire agreement included the release of prisoners of war.
El acuerdo de alto de fuego incluyó la liberación de prisioneros de guerra.
The army made a public statement to announce the withdrawal.
El ejército hizo una declaración pública para anunciar la retirada.
There was a huge explosion as a result of the terrorist attack.
Hubo una gran explosión como resultado del ataque terrorista.
The commander of the insurgency was accused of serious war crimes.
El comandante de la insurgencia fue acusado de graves crímenes de guerra.
Several of the submarine sailors were missing in action.
Varios marineros submarinos desaparecieron en acción.

Conclusion

Hopefully, you have enjoyed this book and will use the knowledge you have learned in various situations in your everyday life. In contrast to other methods of learning foreign languages, the theory in this current usage is that ever-greater topics can be broached so that one's vocabulary can expand. This method relies on the discovery I made of the list of core words from each language. Once these are learned, your conversational learning skills will progress very quickly.

You are now ready to discuss sport and school and office-related topics and this will open up your world to a more satisfying extent. Humans are social creatures and language helps us interact. Indeed, at times, it can keep us alive, such as in war situations. You might find yourself in dangerous situations perhaps as a journalist, military personnel or civilian and you need to be armed with the appropriate vocabulary.

"This is a base for military aircraft only," you may have to tell some people who try to enter a field you are protecting, or know what you are being told when someone says to you, "Welcome to the border crossing." As a journalist on a foreign assignment, you may need to quickly understand what you are being told, such as "The sniper killed the highest-ranking lieutenant." If you are someone negotiating on behalf of the army, you may need to find another lieutenant very quickly. Lives, at times, literally depend on your level of understanding and comprehension.

This unique approach that I first discovered when using this method to learn on my own, will have helped you speak the Spanish language much quicker than any other way.

Basic Grammatical Requirements of the Spanish Language

Present Tense Indicative: Regular Verbs

In the Spanish language all infinitive forms of the verbs end in: "ar", "er", "ir". The verbs are conjugated in the present tense of the indicative form by just adding the following personal endings to the stem of the verb.

	Hablar	**Comer**	**Vivir**
Yo	hablo	como	vivo
Tu	hablas	comes	vives
El, ella, usted	habla	come	vive
Nostro/as	hablamos	comemos	vivemos
Vosotros/as	hablais	comeis	vivis
Ellos, ellas, ustedes	hablan	comen	viven

AR VERBS   **ER VERBS**   **IR VERBS**

The asterick represents irregular verbs.

AR VERBS	ER VERBS	IR VERBS
Comprar - To buy	**Beber** - To drink	**Abrir** - To open
Bailar - To dance	**Comer** - To eat	**Escribir** - To write
Cambiar - To change	**Leer** - To read	**Assistir** - To assist
Desear - To wish	**Creer** - To believe	**Insistir** - To insist
Preguntar - To ask	**Responder** - To respond	**Recibir** - To receive
Trabajar - To work	**Vender** - To sell	***Preferir** - To prefer
Necesitar - To need	**Leer** - To read	***Incluir** - To include
Tomar - To take	***Querer** - To want	***Salir** - To leave
Llegar - To arrive	**Obedecer** - To obey	***Servir** - To serve
Ayudar - To help	***Tener** - To have	***Decir** - To say
Estudiar - To study	**Comprender** - To understand	***Sentir** - To feel
Escuchar - To hear	***Saber** - To know	
Viajar - To travel		
Demorar - To delay		
Terminar - To finish		
Pagar - To pay		

Basic Grammatical Requirements of the Spanish Language

The Articles "the" and "a"

In Spanish, nouns are plural or singular as well as masculine or feminine. For example, the article "the" for Spanish, nouns ending with an *a, e,* and *i* (usually deemed as feminine) is typically *la*. For nouns ending with an *o*, or a consonant, then the noun is generally masculine, and the article is usually *el*. In plural form is *los* for masculine forms and *las* for feminine forms. "The boy" is *el* (the) *niño* (boy), "the girl" is *la niña*, "the boys" are *los niños*, and "the girls" are *las niñas*. ("the house" is *la casa*, "the car" is *el auto*). Although there are exceptions, such as for words that end with *ma, pa,* and *ta*, the article is usually *el*. Plus, some nouns are considered irregular and must be memorized. For example, "the problem" is *el problema* and not *la problema*. Also, the "wall" *la pared* or "the water" *el agua*.

For the article "a" (*un* and *una*), its conjugation is determined by feminine and masculine forms, "a car"—*un auto*, "a house"—*una casa*.

The conjugation for "this" (*esta, este, estos,* and *estas*) and "that" (*ese, esa, esos, esas*) is similar. "This," *este*, is masculine, for example, *este libro* ("this book"). Feminine
is *esta*, for instance, *esta casa* ("this house"). *Estos libros* ("these books") and *estas casas* ("these houses") is the plural form. "That," *ese*, is masculine, that is, *ese libro* (that book). Feminine would be *esa*, for example, *esa silla* ("that chair"). In plural, this is *esos libros* ("those books) and *esas sillas* ("those chairs").

Temporary and Permanent

The different forms of "is" are *es* and *esta*. When referring to a permanent condition, for example, "she is a girl" (*ella es una niña*), you use *es*. For temporary positions, "the girl is doing well today" (*la chica esta muy bien hoy*), you use *esta*. However, *está* is also used to indicate a permanent location, for example, "Spain is located in Europe" / *España está ubicada en Europa*.

"You are" or "are you" could be translated as *estas*, or they could also be translated
as *tú eres*. An example of temporary position is "how are you today?" (*cómo estas hoy*). And another example of temporary position is "you are here"
(*estas aquí*). Another example of permanent position is "are you Mexican?" (*tú eres Mexicano?*) as well as "you are a man!" (*tú eres un hombre!*). Both derive from the verbs *ser* (permanent) and *estar* (temporary).

"I am"—***estoy* and *yo soy*.** *Yo soy* refers to a permanent condition: "I am Italian" / *Yo soy Italiano*. Temporary condition would be "I am at the mall" / *Estoy en el mall*.

"We are"—***somos* (permanent) and *estamos* (temporary).** *Somos Peruvianos* / "we are Peruvian" and *estamos en el parque* / "we are at the park."

"They are"—*son* **(permanent)** *ellos son Chilenos* / "they are Chileans", **and *estan* (temporary)** *ellos estan en el auto* / "they are in the car."

Eso and *esto* are neuter pronouns, meaning they don't have a gender. They usually refer to an idea or an unknown object that isn't specifically named, for example, "that"/ *eso*; "that is"/ *eso es*; "because of that" / *por eso*; "this" / *esto*; "this is good" / *esto es bien;* and "what is this?" / *qué es esto?*

In regards to "my," singular and plural form exists as well, *mi* and *mis*.

"my chair" / *mi silla*
"my chairs" / *mis sillas*

With regard to "your," *tu* and *tus*, the singular is *tu*, as in *tu auto* / "your car," and the plural is *tus* (e.g., *tus autos* / your cars).

Verb Conjugation

The word "I" (*yo*) before a conjugated verb isn't required. For example, *yo necesito saber la fecha* ("I need to know the date") can be said, *Necesito saber la fecha* because *necesito* already means "I need" in conjugated form, although saying *yo* isn't incorrect! The same can also be said with *tú* / *te, el* / *ella, nosotros, ellos* / *ellas*, in which they aren't required to be placed prior to the conjugated verb, but if they are, then it isn't wrong.

Synonyms and Antonyms
There are three ways of describing time.
Vez/veces — "first time" / *primera vez* or "three times" / *tres veces*
Tiempo — "during the time of the dinosaurs" / *durante el tiempo de los dinosaurios*
Hora — "What time is it?" / *Qué hora es?*

Que has four definitions.
"What"—*Que es esto?* / "What is this?"
"Than"—*Estoy mejor que tu* / "I am better than you"
"That"—"I want to say that I am near the house" / *yo quiero decir que estoy acerca de la casa*
"I must" / "I have to"—*Tengo que*. The verb *tener*, "to have," whether it's in conjugated or infinite form, if it is followed by an infinitive verb, then *que* must always follow.

For example: "I have to swim now" / *tengo que nadar ahora*.

There are two ways of describing "so."
"So"—*entonces*. "So I need to know" / *entonces necesito saber*.
"So"—*tan. Eso es tan distante* / "this is so far"

Si and *Sí*
Si (without accent) means "if" / *Sí* (with accent) means "yes"

Basic Grammatical Requirements of the Spanish Language

Tú, Te, Ti and Tu

There are three different forms of how to use the pronoun "you"—*tú*, *te*, and *ti*.

Tú is a subject pronoun (second person of singular), referring to the individual who is doing the action. Unlike in English, it isn't required in Spanish. For example, in "you are here" / *estas aquí*, you aren't required to say *tú estas aquí*.

Te is a direct and indirect object pronoun, the person who is actually affected by the action that is being carried out. But the *te* comes before the verb, for example, "I send you" / *Yo te mando* or "I permit you" / *Yo te permito*. In the event the verb is infinitive, then *te* precedes the verb. For example, in the sentence "I want to follow you" / *quiero seguirte, seguir* and the *te* will connect with the verb and become one word.

Ti is a preposition pronoun, meaning it goes with a preposition (like *para*, *de*, *por*), for example, *para ti* / "for you" or *yo voy a ti* / "I am going to you" (added *a ti*).

Tu without the accent (´) means "your": *tu casa* / "your house."

Tuyo means "yours" and *tuyos* is plural, for example, *el libro es tuyo* / "the book is yours" and "the books are yours" / *los libros son tuyos*.

Ir a + infinitive and yo voy & me voy

In Spanish "to," *a* (pronounced as "ha"), isn't required between the conjugated verb and the infinitive form. For example, *Yo puedo decir* ("I can say"). But in regards to the verb "to go", *ir*, then the preposition *a* must always follow the *ir*, (whether in the conjugated or infinitive form) before connecting with the infinitive verb. For example, *Yo voy a ver* ("I am going to see") or *Yo necesito ir a buscar* ("I need to go to search"). "I go" and "I am going" could either be translated as *yo voy* or *me voy*. *Yo voy* refers to going to a specific place, for example, *yo voy a la tienda* ("I am going to the store"). *Me voy* is going somewhere and not specifying the exact destination, for example, *me voy afuera* ("I am going outside").

Using De

De is one of the most crucial prepositions in the Spanish language. Its most common use is much like the English words "from" and "of," but you will encounter it in other situations as well. It could also mean "than," "in," "with," and "by."

Use *de* when referring to "of" and "from."
"I am from the United States" / *soy de los Estados Unidos*.
"three more days of summer" / *tres más días de verano*.

Another form of *de* is to indicate the possessor.

la casa de Moises / "Moises's house" or "the house of Moises"

las playas de Florida / "Florida's beaches" or "the beaches of Florida"

Another use for *de* is for preposition phrases.

afuera de la casa de tu novia / "outside the house of your girlfriend"
a lado de tu novio / "next to your boyfriend"
alrededor de la picina / "around the pool"

However, if *de* is followed by *el* then both words combine to form *del*. For example, "from the car" / *del auto*, and **not** *de el auto*.

This should cover the most typical uses of *de*. However, there are other uses which haven't been mentioned here.

Using Lo and La

Lo and *La* are used as direct masculine, feminine, and neuter object pronouns, meaning "him," "her," or "it."

In case the verb is conjugated, *lo* and *la* precede the conjugated verb.

"I don't want him to know" / *no lo quiero conocer*
"I don't need her" / *No la necesito*

If the verb is in the infinitive form, then the *lo* and the *la* precede the infinitive verb and connect, creating one word:

"I want to buy it." / *Quiero comprarlo.*
"I want to find it." / *Quiero encontrarlo.*
"I want to see her." / *Quiero verla.*
"I don't want to know him." / *No quiero conocerlo.*
"I don't want to give her." / *No quiero darla.*

Another example of using *lo* in Spanish, is, as the abstract neuter article "the".

*   "the best of Charlie Chaplin" / *lo mejor de Charlie Chaplin* (since "best" is the abstract neuter noun).

Reflexive Form

In the Spanish language we use *me, te,* and *se* in relation to the reflexive form of a verb, which will be preceding or proceeding that verb, and set as a prefix or suffix. For example, the verb "to wash" - *lavar*. "I wash myself" - *me lavo* / "you wash yourself" - *te lavas* / "he washed himself" - *se lava.*

In the infinitive form it connects as a suffix: "I want to wash myself" - *quiero lavarme* / "you wash yourself" - *quieres lavarte* / "he washed himself" - *quiere lavarse.*

Congratulations! Now You Are on Your Own!

If you merely absorb the required three hundred and fifty words in this book, you will then have acquired the basis to become conversational in Spanish! After memorizing these three hundred and fifty words, this conversational foundational basis that you have just gained will trigger your ability to make improvements in conversational fluency at an amazing speed! However, in order to engage in quick and easy conversational communication, you need a special type of basics, and this book will provide you with just that.

Unlike the foreign language learning systems presently used in schools and universities, along with books and programs that are available on the market today, that focus on *everything* but being conversational, *this* method's sole focus is on becoming conversational in Spanish as well as any other language. Once you have successfully mastered the required words in this book, there are two techniques that if combined with these essential words, can further enhance your skills and will result in you improving your proficiency tenfold. *However*, these two techniques will only succeed *if* you have completely and successfully absorbed the three hundred and fifty words. *After* you establish the basis for fluent communications by memorizing these words, you can enhance your conversational abilities even more if you use the following two techniques.

The first step is to attend a Spanish language class that will enable you to sharpen your grammar. You will gain additional vocabulary and learn past and present tenses, and if you apply these skills that you learn in the class, together with the three hundred and fifty words that you have previously memorized, you will be improving your conversational skills tenfold. You will notice that, conversationally, you will succeed at a much higher rate than any of your classmates. A simple second technique is to choose Spanish subtitles while watching a movie. If you have successfully mastered and grasped these three hundred and fifty words, then the combination of the two—those words along with the subtitles—will aid you considerably in putting all the grammar into perspective, and again, conversationally, you will improve tenfold.

Once you have established a basis of quick and easy conversation in Spanish with those words that you just attained, every additional word or grammar rule you pick up from there on will be gravy. And these additional words or grammar rules can be combined with the three hundred and fifty words, enriching your conversational abilities even more. Basically, after the research and studies I've conducted with my method over the years, I came to the

Congratulations! Now You Are on Your Own!

conclusion that in order to become conversational, you first must learn the words and *then* learn the grammar.

The Spanish language is compatible with the mirror translation technique. Likewise, with *this* language, you can use this mirror translation technique in order to become conversational, enabling you to communicate even more effortlessly. Mirror translation is the method of translating a phrase or sentence, word for word from English to Spanish, by using these imperative words that you have acquired through this program (such as the sentences I used in this book). Latin languages, Middle Eastern languages, and Slavic languages, along with a few others, are also compatible with the mirror translation technique. Though you won't be speaking perfectly proper and precise Spanish, you will still be fully understood and, conversation-wise, be able to get by just fine.

NOTE FROM THE AUTHOR

Thank you for your interest in my work. I encourage you to share your overall experience of this book by posting a review. Your review can make a difference! Please feel free to describe how you benefited from my method or provide creative feedback on how I can improve this program. I am constantly seeking ways to enhance the quality of this product, based on personal testimonials and suggestions from individuals like you. In order to post a review, please check with the retailer of this book.

Thanks and best of luck,

Yatir Nitzany

www.ingramcontent.com/pod-product-compliance
Lightning Source LLC
Chambersburg PA
CBHW050323120526
44592CB00014B/2025